What the Rich Know That the Poor Don't Know

8 Secrets of the Truly Rich

How You Can Create Material Wealth and Gain Spiritual Abundance at the Same Time

Happy Birthday Lawrence! Papa 11/08/12

This is God's Recruitment Manual:
He Is Raising a New Breed of Millionaires Who Are Simple, Loving and Generous... Join Now!

BO SANCHEZ

National Bestselling Author of *Simplify and Live the Good Life* and *Simplify and Create Abundance*

SHEPHERD'S VOICE

"Bo Sanchez's *8 Secrets of the Truly Rich* balances our views concerning material wealth. It helps us appreciate God's gifts as means to multiply goodness in the world. May this book enlighten readers on the real value of money and its relation to the spiritual life."

+ Ricardo J. Cardinal Vidal
Archbishop of Cebu

"Being poor is not an acceptable excuse. There is nothing wrong with aspiring to be materially comfortable. Bo's book inspires us to work hard and aim high to be wealthy in the true sense of the word.

Bo shows the way! A good read!"

— Socorro C. Ramos
Founder and General Manager, National Bookstore

"*8 Secrets of the Truly Rich* will inspire his readers to have the right attitude towards wealth, and give them practical tips on how to achieve financial success. This book is a combination of Kiyosaki's *Rich Dad, Poor Dad* infused with Bo Sanchez's humor and down-to-earth style. Talk about value for money! Practice what you preach, indeed."

— Bernadette Sembrano
TV Host, ABS-CBN

"Bo Sanchez demolishes the myths that equate wealth with materialism, and having money with being rich. He demonstrates how Christians and everyone else can and should strive to be wealthy, provided that there is social and economic justice and cooperation. He strikes the right chords when he pushes right attitudes, hard work and hits hard at the cultural baggage that hinders Filipino entrepreneurship."

— Gerry Ablaza
CEO, Globe Telecoms

"Bo Sanchez has never lacked for things to preach about daily.... In his latest book, he preaches on wealth. He shows that as in all good things, the true value of wealth lies not in possessing it but in giving it away.

And that the only wealth that really matters are the riches that can be stored in our Father's Kingdom in heaven."

+ Gaudencio B. Cardinal Rosales
Archbishop of Manila

"This book is a good guide to discovering hidden treasures in our people. ... Let us chart our path to prosperity by developing the excellence of our people including the poorest of the poor in our country without losing our anchor on strong values and principles."

— Tony Meloto
Gawad Kalinga

"Bo says, 'Money isn't the most important thing in the world. But money affects every important thing in the world.' Statements like these make Bo's book — every chapter of it — very tempting to read. Catchy. Reflective. You have the power to transform the world: Start it... with yourself!"

+ Angel N. Lagdameo
Archbishop of Jaro, Iloilo

"I used to think that wanting more than what you need is greed, but Bro. Bo Sanchez has given me a new perspective — that wanting more to be able to give more is God's wish for us. Thanks, Bro. Bo. I'll continue gazing upon the Lord."

— Julie Gandiongco
Founder, Julie's Bakeshop

"Bo Sanchez has done it again! This book is an excellent combination of personal experiences, well-researched investment information and sound spiritual guidance for all of us. I congratulate the author for this wonderful book, for daring us to pursue our dream to be truly rich without losing our heart and selling our soul to the devil."

— Jose Concepçion, Jr.
Chairman of the Board, RFM Corporation

"This book is like manna from heaven, a gift from God, delivered so beautifully by Bo. It came at a time when I needed answers to my prayers, solutions to my financial woes.... From the very first page of this book, I got hooked. After reading this, you will learn to protect yourself financially.... I now commit to be wealthy so that I can help more people and make their lives better. Thank you, Bo, for your words of wisdom!"

— Tintin Bersola-Babao
TV Host, ABS-CBN

PREFACE

This Book Is About Changing Your Inner Software

I've met many Filipinos who have been programmed to be poor.

Their very self-definition shouts to the universe, "I'm poor and I'll always be poor." This twisted core identity, plus insane religious beliefs about money, are like invisible prison bars that keep many Filipinos locked in poverty.

My mission is to free you from that prison.

For over 25 years, I've been working among the poor, living in their homes and helping them get out of poverty.

I've found out that no matter how much money people receive, unless they change their inner program, nothing happens. They will indeed remain poor forever.

Friend, do you have a money problem?

Read carefully: 90 percent of your money problems are mind problems.

People are not poor because they have no money. That's merely the result, not the cause of poverty.

Filipinos are poor because of a lethal combination of three giant monsters of poverty.

<u>First, we really don't want to be rich.</u>

As shocking as this may sound, it's true. Externally, we seem to want to be rich, but internally, we're deeply conflicted in our unconscious desires. Because our distorted core beliefs about ourselves, plus our crazy religious beliefs about money, chain us to the prison of poverty.

<u>Second, we're financially stupid.</u> (That's putting it *mildly*.)

We don't know how money works. And we don't know how money grows. So we lose whatever little we have. Because what we know about money comes from friends and relatives who don't have money themselves — and so, they teach us from their ignorance. And school never taught us how money worked either because teachers didn't know.

Third, we insist on walking, instead of riding, vehicles towards wealth.

Even if there are hundreds — no thousands — of vehicles around us. In the pages of this book, I will explain what these vehicles are.

Friend, do you want to gain material and spiritual wealth at the same time?

Then, read on as if you were a drowning person, and this book was your oxygen. If you do this and apply all that you learn, I promise that you can solve your mind problems — which can lead you to solving your money problems.

DEDICATION

- I'm writing this book to the father who wakes up at night, wondering how to earn more money to pay for his kids' rising tuition fees.
- I'm writing to the mother who gets acidic in her stomach every time the phone rings, because creditors are hounding her for late debt payments.
- I'm writing to desperate parents who've been working abroad for years — away from their growing children — and yet are wondering why they still haven't saved anything.
- I'm writing to the married daughter who wants to help in her aging mother's medical expenses but can't because her salary isn't even enough for her own family's needs.
- I'm writing to the single man in his 30s whose girlfriend is asking when they'd get married, but can't even plan one because he's still paying for his younger siblings' schooling.
- I'm writing to the supervisor who's tired of living from paycheck to paycheck, without any savings whatsoever.
- I'm writing to the employee whose salary isn't even enough for her transportation to the office because of all the debt payments being deducted from her each month.
- I'm writing to the manager who is 50 years old and who wants to retire early but can't — because she has debts that will shrink her retirement pay to almost nothing.
- I'm writing to the 65-year-old retiree who has to live on his monthly SSS pension that can't even pay for his daily medication.
- I'm writing to the spiritual leader who wants to help her members who are poor and who often ask for her help, but can't because her income isn't enough.
- I'm writing to the entrepreneur who's failing in his business and wonders what he's done wrong and what he should do next.
- I'm writing to the Filipinos who are tired of the Philippines as a Third World country and dream of a First World Philippines for their children and grandchildren.
- I'm writing to the spiritual person who is torn by his desire to help others financially, and his longing to remain pure, simple, detached, trusting and non-materialistic in his attitude towards life.

Friend, I dedicate this book to you.

What the Rich Know That the Poor Don't Know

8 Secrets of the Truly Rich

How You Can Create Material Wealth and Gain Spiritual Abundance at the Same Time

ISBN- 978-971-93671-2-3

BO SANCHEZ

National Bestselling author of *Simplify and Live the Good Life* and *Simplify and Create Abundance*

7th Reprinting, January 2012

Address requests for information to:
SHEPHERD'S VOICE PUBLICATIONS, INC.
#60 Chicago St., Cubao, Quezon City, Philippines 1109
P.O. Box 1331 Quezon City Central Post Office
1153 Quezon City
Tel. No. (+632) 725-9999 Fax. No. (632) 727-5615, 725-1230
e-mail: sales@shepherdsvoice.com.ph

Cover Design and Layout design by Rey de Guzman
Cover Photo by Dakila Angeles

TABLE OF CONTENTS

FOREWORD

Is It Possible to Have the Wealth of a Millionaire and the Heart of a Monk?

Then the Lord your God will make you most prosperous
in all the work of your hands...
Deuteronomy 30:9

This is unlike any other book you've ever read about money.

In these pages, I propose to you a way of life where you can be open to money and wealth, yet your soul is free from greed and materialism.

I propose to you a way of life where you create material abundance yet remain detached, pure, and loving in your heart and inner purpose.

Is is possible, you ask, to have the wealth of a millionaire and the heart of a monk at the same time?

My answer is a resounding yes!

I'm not going to kid you: It will be difficult.

But is that surprising? Nothing of great achievement comes easy.

Why Be Rich Anyway?

This question is crucial.

In fact, there are religious people out there ready to crucify me now — because they think there is only one reason why people want to be rich: because of greed.

"What has happened to Bo?" they ask, "He's gone over to the devil's side. He's now preaching materialism."

Friend, I can't and will never preach materialism.

Believe me, I've seen materialism in the depths of my soul and smelled its stench. I've seen it at work in the hearts of those I try to help every day, and I saw how materialism eats her children alive. Materialism promises heaven but delivers hell. It's a faceless monster that destroys persons, families and nations.

No, wealth can never answer the deepest longings of our soul.
Only love can do that.
Only God can do that.
So why is a preacher like me writing a book about money?

I Don't Want You to Be Rich; I Want You to Be *Truly* Rich

Why stop at being rich?

Why not go all the way to become truly rich?

When you're truly rich, you're not only wealthy with your money. You're wealthy in all other areas of your life: love, family, spirituality...

For example, I don't even look rich at all.

Despite now having 16 sources of income flowing to my life, I still live a simple life. Because I want to!

My wife and I still live in a tiny house built on a 65-square-meter property. It's so small; I can close the windows and open the fridge and you'd think we had centralized air-conditioning. I tell our visitors to visit us two by two so that they can fit.

But according to Thomas Stanley in his best-selling book, *The Millionaire Next Door,* most millionaires in America live in simple homes located in simple neighborhoods.

Our home is in a third-class subdivision that doesn't even have running water. Yes, there are places forgotten by time in civilized Manila. Dig under our street, and there are no water pipes under the ground — just like in Ancient Mesopotamia. We have to order water at P150 per delivery truck.

So we hate our home and neighborhood, right?

Wrong.

I cannot describe to you how we love it here.

The Lifestyle of the Rich and Faithful

I've learned to measure wealth not just by how much money I have, but by how much of that money is controlled by love.

Let me tell you my story.

When I was 12 years old, I had a spiritual conversion.

I met God and He rocked my world.

Part of that conversion was tithing.

I decided to give a tithe or 10 percent of my daily allowance to God.

That was difficult.

After all, Mom gave me P2 a day — not enough for an ice cream cone, which was P2.50 per scoop. So giving 20 centavos was a real sacrifice.

But I did it and learned a lifestyle that would never leave me to this day.

In the Old Testament, people were called to tithe, but in the New Testament, we're called to give from our joyful hearts. And when you're joyful, you tend to give more!

After 28 years of giving, I now earn enough to the point that I give 40 percent of my income to God and to the poor. (Hey, I know I'll lose a few rewards in heaven for telling you how much I give. But I don't care. I want to inspire people to give more to God and the poor.)

This is why I say I'm truly rich: because I'm a giver.

I'm far from becoming a millionaire in dollar figures. (One day, I'll reach that point, too. Just wait.) But it's of secondary importance to me.

Here's my real dream: To do a reverse tithe.

From giving 40 percent of my income to God and the poor, I want to earn so much that I can give 90 percent — and live on the remaining 10 percent. (Yes, I've got it all plotted out, written down in my 15-page Dream Book that I've been reading each morning for 10 years now. It's been incredibly accurate. If God blesses my business plans, I'll be able to do that by the year 2037. That's only a few decades from now. That's why I believe God has indeed given us the power to create our destiny.)

Hey, this is me. I'm not in any way imposing my dream on you.

I'm not even saying that you should give 40 percent of your income to God and the poor. That's my personal decision. My life has been so involved in ministry and service, I know its many needs. That's why I made that my dream.

But this is my challenge to you: Earn to give.

And it's true, God will bless the giver more than he can imagine.

You've Been Tricked

So friends, I've conned you.

I've tricked you into buying this book.

This book isn't about being rich only.

This book is about being rich so that you can give your wealth to God and let Him do what He wishes with it.

The title of the book should be *8 Secrets of the Rich Who Believe That the Ultimate Purpose of Wealth Is to Love.*

Okay, that's too long.

That's why I didn't use it.

Friends, this book isn't about greed. It's about the opposite of greed.

This book isn't about materialism. It's deeply spiritual.

This book isn't even a book but God's Recruitment Manual.

God is recruiting people who will join a new force in this world.

I call this group God's New Breed of True Millionaires.

It's really up to you if you want to join.

I'm not going to fool you.

It's going to be tough. It will require your unflinching commitment. You'll get bloodied up. You'll get mangled. You'll wake up early in the morning and sleep late at night. You'll do so many things out of your comfort zone, you'll forget what the phrase "comfort zone" means.

If you've got what it takes, then welcome.

You're in for a great journey.

In the next page is a membership form for God's New Breed of True Millionaires. Fill it out. Sign it. And "give" it to God. (Pin it on your wall so you see it every day.)

By the way, I submitted my application papers 10 years ago.

And in the next few pages, I'm going to tell you the thrilling experience of how I became truly rich.

God's New Breed of True Millionaires

MEMBERSHIP FORM

I apply as a member of God's True Millionaires...

____

(Your Name)

The True Millionaire's Prayer

Today, I ask You to bless me so that I may become a blessing.
Lord, I commit myself to enrich others.
But because I cannot give what I do not have,
I commit myself to become rich.
I commit myself to serve You and to serve the poor with my wealth.
Today, I open myself to the abundance of Your universe.
Use me as Your channel of love.
Give me the ability to create wealth that will bless the world.
Increase my financial wisdom and expand my territories.
I place my life in Your hands. Amen.

My Financial Goal:

____

(Monthly Income)

Date when this goal will happen:

____

____

Member's Signature

____

Date Today

Instructions: Members of **God's New Breed of Millionaires** *should say this prayer and pray for their financial goal EVERY DAY until it is fulfilled.*

INTRODUCTION

My Journey from Medieval Assisi to Present-Day Manila

I always like enumerating the significant moments of my youth:

I wrote my first book at age 20.

I founded my first organization at age 14.

I began preaching at age 13.

I had my spiritual conversion at age 12.

And I was toilet-trained at age one, but that has nothing to do with what I'm about to say in this book.

As you can see, my teen years were slightly different than most people. While boys my age were busy playing with the primitive versions of video games (Pacman), I was going to the barrios organizing small prayer meetings and giving retreats in schools.

Yes, I was a freak.

Especially when I read the story of St. Francis of Assisi.

I was only 13. All of a sudden, Superman was no longer my hero. Francis was.

I wanted to love like Francis, serve like Francis, look like Francis and smell like Francis. I remember my favorite attire — old brown sandals, tattered jogging pants and a dirty-white T-shirt. To be consistent with that look, I rarely took a bath and gave up the use of any kind of underarm deodorant because I thought that was vanity.

So you could imagine the powerful impact I had on people's lives.

Whenever I entered the room, people knew.

If you read the biography of some saints, you'd read that some of them had the odor of sanctity — a beautiful, sweet-smelling fragrance that made people feel God's Presence.

Well, I had odor all right and I brought people to their knees.

A Lover of the Poor

By age 15, I was already living in the slums, befriending the poor, eating their food, sleeping in their dilapidated homes and celebrating life with them.

I also worked on filthy sidewalks, playing with street kids and befriending old, drunk, homeless men. I'd lead them in prayer, give them Bibles and a piece of bread.

I was ready to do anything for God.

During those years, I didn't think about money, I didn't care about money and I didn't desire money.

Why?

I figured that I'd be a lifelong celibate for God.

I was going to serve others as a single man for the rest of my life.

So living hand-to-mouth and sleeping on the sidewalk was actually a sweet fantasy in my mind. Saints lived this way, and I thought to myself, "So, why shouldn't I live this way, too?"

I owned nothing except what was in my pocket: a small New Testament Bible and a wooden rosary. Oh yes, my toothbrush, too.

You see, I also had this incomplete belief: that the only way to love the poor was to become poor myself. I didn't understand that this was only half of the equation. I forgot that the goal of loving the poor is to help them stop being poor.

But that's going ahead of my story.

The Missionary Life

When I finished college, I never got a regular job.

I kept on serving and shunned all material things or its pursuit.

I built communities, wrote Christian magazines, published spiritual books and organized a home for the aged.

How did I survive?

My lay community, Light of Jesus, gave me a small salary—which was more than enough for a single man with simple needs. I never bought clothes, wore whatever was given to me and walked to where I needed to go.

To make travel easier, I bought a homemade, garage-assembled WWII jeep.

It was perfect.

Perfect for growing my hamstring muscles because I had to push it almost every day — because it usually didn't like to start.

Each day, I lived by faith....

Faith that my jeep wouldn't explode into a thousand junk pieces all over EDSA.

Faith that I had enough gas to bring me home each night.

Faith that I wouldn't die of hypertension because of my jeep's surprises.

Money Was Evil

At that time, I basically gave my money away.

One day, someone gave me P50,000.

After a few days, I met a friend and I asked him, "Do you need P50,000?" He said yes and I gave it to him. Just like that.

I also never saved anything.

I figured that saving for tomorrow meant that I wasn't trusting God.

I was a complete ignoramus about money, and proud of it. In my mind, I asked, "Why study the devil? Why bother knowing his instruments?"

Basically, I saw money as evil.

Business was greed.

Thinking of money was sin.

Wealth was excess baggage that prevented people from going to heaven.

And I really pitied businessmen!

Imagine, all they do is think about how to make money the whole day.

Gosh, their souls were in danger of the fires of hell.

As for me, I'd just trust God and He'd supply all my needs.

Let me give you my favorite example.

One day, my hair was getting too groovy for a preacher and I needed a haircut.

My problem was I had no money.

So I asked God, "Lord, I need a haircut."

That night, someone in the prayer meeting went to my side, pushed an envelope into my pocket, and said, "God wanted me to give this to you."

When I went home, I opened it and saw P10,000.

The next day, I went to the barbershop and asked the barber, "Give me the most expensive haircut in the world. With highlights of blue and pink. The works!"

That was how I lived my life for 18 long years.

I was living in medieval Assisi, begging with St. Francis on the streets. It was a beautiful life — the life of a celibate who embraced Lady Poverty as his bride.

But once in a while, I saw harsh reality zap through my imagination.

Reality Pokes Its Finger

This event is chiseled in my memory.

I was never the same again after it happened.

After one prayer meeting, a woman with her small daughter approached me and asked, "Bo, can you pray over me?"

"Of course," I smiled, "what can I pray for?"

"Tomorrow is the last day for my daughter's enrollment and I have no money..." She quietly sobbed, clutching her daughter to her waist.

She explained that she had been praying to God but it seemed as though nothing was happening. "Bo, please pray over me that God will increase my faith!"

I became curious. "How much money do you need, exactly?" I asked.

"Seven hundred," she said.

"Seven hundred? Seven hundred only?" I couldn't believe my ears.

"It's a monthly installment thing," she explained.

At that precise moment, I wanted to pull out my wallet and give her the 700 bucks. I wanted to say, "Look, sister, I don't have to pray over you. Here's the money and go home!"

But I couldn't.

No matter how much I wanted to.

Because as I stood there in front of her, I knew that I only had P20 in my wallet. Twenty pesos!

So what did I do?

I prayed over her.

After I laid my hands on her, she thanked me and bid me farewell.

Believe me, I've done a lot of difficult things in my life.

But one of the most difficult was watching this lady and her daughter walk out of that room empty-handed.

When they disappeared through the door, I sat down on a chair and felt a deep pain inside. A prayer formed in my heart, "Lord, I don't want this to ever happen again. Oh, to have money to help others! Help me help them."

Fast forward to a few years later. I now earn enough to send a few poor children to school. And the feeling is incredible.

But I'm going ahead of the story.

Like a 10-Wheeler Truck

When I was 30 years old, I was already living in Anawim,[1] a home we built for the poorest of the poor. It was built on a five-hectare property with 10 homes, welcoming especially the abandoned elderly. Together with wonderful friends who served the poor, we lived in total dependence on God for our daily food.

In Anawim, I lived in a bamboo hut with eight orphans.

That experience was one of the richest seasons in my life.

I fell in love with the kids and felt I could live with them forever.

Again, this was medieval Assisi and St. Francis was my guide.

But it was also at that exact time when something was happening in my soul.

I felt God was calling me to get married. (How I finally came to that conclusion after years of indecision is found in my book *How to Find Your One True Love.*)

That was when the veil of medieval Assisi was lifted and reality hit me like a 10-wheeler truck. Wham!

I was back in present-day Manila.

How in the world could I get married? I had no money.

Nothing.

[1] A Hebrew word which means "The poor of the Lord"

Nada.
Kaput.
Zilcho.
Reality hit hard.

The Wedding of the Century

So for a year, I scrambled to save money, at least enough for a simple wedding.

When I thought I had enough, I planted one knee before this pretty girl I was courting in my office and asked for her hand in marriage.

And on my 32nd birthday, I married her.

Our wedding was simple. Some have five, 10 or 20 people in their entourage. We had 80. Because I wanted to include my orphans, the Anawim elderly, our community kids, etc. And our guests? Oh, not much. Only a thousand people.

Thankfully, most of the gowns were gifts, my *barong tagalog* was a gift, the bridal car was lent, and even the wedding rings were gifts.

And our reception for a thousand guests? Potluck.

No kidding.

What could have cost me a million pesos, I spent only P100,000.

Because that was all I had.

But my wedding was like a jarring wake-up call to me — a call to harsh reality.

Was money really this important to a married person?

It was a brutal awakening.

I was no longer in peaceful, picturesque, mountain-cool Assisi.

I was now in smog-filled, horn-blowing, hot and humid Manila.

I was no longer a single man doing mission work and living by faith.

I was now married and I needed money. Fast.

Living Simply in Good and Bad Times

My wife and I lived in a rented apartment for two years.

And like many newlyweds, we searched for ways to make my small salary reach the end of the month.

We used old, borrowed furniture.

We had no air-conditioning to save on electricity.

We bought margarine instead of butter.

We chose ugly, coarse toilet paper instead of the smooth premium brand.

And we searched for the cheapest places for our weekly romantic dates.

We only ate in fast-foods (collecting discount coupons), had picnics in nearby parks, watched free theater plays in a university, and rented a movie for P15 so we could enjoy cuddle time on our borrowed couch.

But here's another reason why we were living simply: Before getting married, I told my would-be bride that I'd like to continue giving a part of my income to God and to the poor. At that time, I was giving 20 percent. And she agreed wholeheartedly.

But I'm not going to hide this truth from you: Money was tight and we fought over it. Not often, but they erupted from time to time.

Usually, it was because she wanted to buy something for the house (a tea cup, a tiny décor or something like that), and I felt it was a waste of money. With my St. Francis spirituality, everything was a waste of money. Many times, I hurt my wife because I was so stingy.

Sometimes in tears, she'd tell me, "Bo, you're so generous to others, we give 20 percent of our income away. But you're not generous to your wife."

Ouch. Why does the truth hurt?

I realized that if I wanted to keep on giving the way I wanted to — and have a happy family — I also needed to earn much more!

I Searched for Mentors

The first thing I did was read everything I could read about money.

But here's the big difference: I read these books with the eyes of my faith. (Medieval Assisi was no longer my world, but it still lived in my heart—and that was good.) I rejected greed in all its forms. I threw away materialism when I saw its ugly shadow. And I only accepted information that could be baptized into our service for God.

So strong was my conviction that materialism destroys a person, I knew that wealth wasn't the answer. It had to be much bigger than wealth.

Here's the second thing that I did: in my work, I met rich people who broke my old stereotypes of rich people. They weren't greedy at all.

In fact, they were incredibly loving and phenomenal human beings.

And they were extremely generous! This was how they viewed their wealth: They earned money so that they could give more to God and His poor.

So I spent time with these True Millionaires.

I had lunch with them.

I picked their brains.

I asked questions.

I took down notes.

I even videotaped our conversations.

Friends, what I learned from these conversations are the eight secrets that the truly rich do which the poor don't do.

Finally, I immediately applied them in my life.

And what has happened over the past years has been nothing but spectacular.

Where I Am Now

In one sense, this book isn't about me.

This book is about my True Millionaire friends who generously shared their secrets on how they became truly rich and loved at the same time.

But I'm sure you'd like to know what has happened to me financially.

As I mentioned, I now enjoy 16 sources of income. These are small investments and small businesses. They're giving me tiny trickles of income. But put them together and I have more than enough that I can give 40 percent of my income to God and live on the 60 percent. (Actually, I live on 30 percent, because I reinvest the other 30 percent back into my businesses.)

This Book Isn't for Everyone

In that sense, this book isn't for everyone.

It's not for people who don't want to get rich.

That would include celibates, religious people in congregations, and missionaries working in the boondocks. That would include very special people who have consecrated themselves to sacrificial poverty. (I know a number of them and I have the highest admiration for them.)

This book isn't also for people who are content with where they are. I've met people who tell me, "Bo, as long as we can eat three meals a day, I'm happy. I don't want the stress of learning anything new. Anyway, I can serve others without being rich, right?"

Of course! You can bless the poor through your talents, your time, your friendship. And I respect people who want to remain in their income level.

Life is like a doughnut shop. There's a doughnut for everyone. Some like it with peanut butter (yes!), others with chocolate, still others with strawberry, and a few strange people like it with coconut.

But for the rest of you who want freedom from your money problems...

For the rest of you who want the freedom to help your loved ones financially...

For the rest of you who dream of a rich Philippines by becoming rich yourself...

For the rest of you who want to create material wealth and spiritual abundance at the same time...

This book is for you.

You Can Be Rich

Because you can be rich.

Yes, you can get out of debt, save enough for the future, be very generous to the poor and God's work.

So who's stopping you?

Here's the answer: YOU.

No one else can stop you.

Not your family, not your friends, not the government, not the poverty of the country. And God?

He won't stop you either. Why would He? He invented wealth.

That's why I'm writing to you today.

Here's my promise: If you learn these *8 Secrets of the Truly Rich* — and apply them into your life, you'll change your financial future forever.

Why am I so confident that these principles will work for you?
Because I've seen them at work in my life.
Because I've seen them at work in the lives of countless others.
Because these principles are laws that rule God's universe.

There is a science of getting rich, and it is an exact science, like algebra or arithmetic. There are certain laws which govern the process of acquiring riches, and once these laws are learned and obeyed by anyone, that person will get rich with mathematical certainty.

— Wallace Wattles

Turn the page and begin your journey to true riches.

1 SECRET

Be Totally Responsible for Your Success

I have now given you a choice between a blessing and a curse. When all these things have happened to you... you will remember the choice I gave you.
— Deuteronomy 30:1

Life is a choice.

If you're being blessed 90 percent of the time, it's because you chose to be blessed.

If you're being cursed 90 percent of the time, it's because you chose to be cursed.

You have more power than you think you have.

Friend, don't be shocked, but you have the power to create the life you want.

Here's the truth: You created the life that you are living right now.

So if you don't like your job, you're responsible.

And if you're buried in debt right now, you're accountable.

And if you're overweight, it's your fault.

And if you're not happy, you're responsible.

I'm not saying you're to blame for all the things that have happened to you.

But you're responsible. That means you're in charge.

If you don't want your situation, change it.

If you can't change your situation, change your attitude towards your situation.

But unless you change, nothing happens.

Bottom line, it's really all up to you.

Be totally responsible for your success.

CHAPTER 1

Stop the Blame

Things do not change; we change.
— Henry David Thoreau

Permanently poor people blame their poverty on everything else but themselves.

And it's so easy to do that.

Because a billion different things affect our money.

If you wanted to, you could blame your poverty on suicide bombers from Afghanistan, the thinning of the ozone layer or the fact that the King of Saudi Arabia fought with his wife the day before an OPEC meeting — which skewed up the oil prices.

You could blame your poverty on your alcoholic father, your overprotective grandmother, or the childhood trauma of listening to Frank Sinatra music over and over again because it was your mother's favorite music.

You could blame practically anything.

But if you keep on blaming your financial condition on things outside yourself, you'll never become rich. Why? Because within every problem is the solution. So if you believe that the problem is outside you, then you don't control the solution.

Only when you say, "I'm the problem," can you say, "I'm the solution."

If you say, "These greedy capitalists keep me poor!" then the solution is in their hands, not in yours. In effect, you're saying that when these capitalists stop becoming greedy, then you'll start becoming rich.

Blame robs you of your power to determine your life.

Remember, the quality of your finances is determined by your choices in life. And unless you stop blaming others and start taking responsibility for your poverty, you'll always remain poor.

And for comic relief — but also to show you our tendency to blame — let me quote some real-life, actual statements found on insurance forms...

- "I collided with a stationary truck coming the other way."

- "A pedestrian hit me and went under the car."

- "The guy was all over the road. I had to swerve a number of times before I hit him."

- "I pulled away from the side of the road, glanced at my mother-in-law and headed over the embankment." (Gee, was she that ugly?)

- "As I approached the intersection, a sign suddenly appeared in place where no stop sign had ever appeared before. I was unable to stop in time to avoid the accident." (Magic. Miracle.)

- "An invisible car came out of nowhere, struck my car and vanished." (Mmm. I've heard of ghost ships. But a ghost car?)

- "My car was legally parked as it backed into the other vehicle."

- "The pedestrian had no idea which direction to run, so I ran over him." (Yes, undecided people are a pest. Kill them all.)

That's human nature. Always looking for someone to blame.
But unless you stop doing that, you'll always be poor.

Stop the blame.

Truly Rich Principle:
Blame robs you of your power to determine your life.

CHAPTER 2

Stop Blaming the Government for Your Poverty

Ninety-nine percent of all failures come from people who have a habit of making excuses.
— George Washington Carver

This chapter is specifically written for my fellow Pinoys.

Because this has become our national pastime. We like blaming our personal financial misery on our government.

One day, I was talking to a friend of mine. Over a cup of coffee, he blurted out in exasperation to me, "Brother Bo, do you know why I'm poor?" He didn't wait for my answer. He said, "It's our (blip) government! From the (blip) policeman on the street to the (blip) President of the Philippines, they're all (blip) corrupt. This (blip) country is going to the dogs because we're being run by a bunch of (blip) thieves!"

If he'd stopped cursing, we'd have shortened our conversation by half.

But I needed to correct a graver mistake.

I said, "Is that the reason why you're poor?"

"Of course!" his nostrils flared, "I hate those (blip) politicians!"

"Then can you explain to me why your next-door neighbor Henry is getting richer no matter who sits in Malacañang? In the past three presidencies, your neighbor built one small business after another. Did he have a different set of presidents, a different set of senators and congressmen than you had?"

My friend was caught off guard. For a moment he just stared at me, not knowing what hit him.

He was probably used to people agreeing with him all the time, even joining him in talking about the muck and grime of our politicians.

Well, I think that's a total waste of my energy.

Personally, I'd rather go to work, build businesses, create jobs and bless the world — than sit around cursing the government. Anyone can curse the dark. But it takes a special person to light a small candle in that darkness.

Don't blame the government for your poverty.

When you blame them, you'll constantly wait for your salvation from the government. But friend, the government won't save you.

Don't wait for prosperity from any politician or any form of government.

If you want prosperity, you've got to go and create it yourself.

Only you — and God working in you — can create the wealth you want.

Stop blaming the government for your poverty.

Truly Rich Principle:
Don't wait for prosperity from the government. If you want prosperity, you've got to go and create it yourself. Only you—and God working in you — can create the wealth you want.

CHAPTER 3

Stop Blaming Your Family for Your Poverty

You can't hire someone else to do your pushups for you.
— Jim Rohn

One day, I was talking to a mother in her 40s.

She told me, "I was born in a poor family. My father is poor, my mother is poor, our grandparents are poor, all our uncles and aunts are poor, even our dog is poor... That's why I'll be poor forever."

I shook my head and said, "There's a slight problem with your logic. Do you know who else can say the exact same story?"

"Who?" she asked.

"Henry Sy, Lucio Tan, John Gokongwei..."

"But Bo, they're not counted!" she objected. "They're Chinese!"

"So? Even worse. At one point, they couldn't speak our language. These three men started with manual labor. And except for Henry Sy who finished in Far Eastern University, the other two couldn't even finish college."

Henry Sy, a penniless 12-year-old boy when he arrived on the shores of the Philippines, is now owner of the SM empire and the 14th richest man in South East Asia.

Lucio Tan, who at one time owned nothing else but the shirt on his back, is now the richest industrialist in the country, and has a net worth of $1.5 billion.

John Gokongwei, former market vendor and *bodegero,* is now head of JG Summit, the largest conglomerate in the Philippines.

If you want to get out of poverty, nothing can stop you.

Not your corrupt government or your family lineage.

Stop blaming your family for your poverty.

Truly Rich Principle:
If you want to get out of poverty, nothing can stop you. Not your corrupt government or your family lineage.

CHAPTER 4

Stop Blaming the Devil for Your Poverty

We have met the enemy and he is us.
— Pogo

Ferdie, a lean man in his mid-30s, approached me after one of our prayer meetings. One look at him and I felt pity for him already. He had dark circles around his eyes and pale skin. He looked perfect for cheap zombie movies.

"Brother Bo, I've had so much bad luck in my life!" he said. "Last year, I lost my job. That's my fifth job in three years. Now, I'm buried in credit card debt... Oh, what bad luck!"

"I don't believe in bad luck," I said, "I believe we create our luck."

"You don't understand. Someone told me that there was evil in my house and I need to remove them."

"Evil?" I asked, "What do you mean?" For a moment, I wondered if my zombie theory was accurate.

Ferdie said, "A Charismatic friend visited my home last month. She saw my souvenirs from my trips and saw evil behind these objects. A doll from Bali, a feng shui mirror, a Buddha figurine from China.... She said the devil is attacking me because of these poisonous objects in my home. If I removed them, she said I'll be blessed and receive financial blessings again. So I threw them all away."

I asked, "And what happened?"

"Nothing yet," he groaned.

"You've had five jobs in three years, right?" I asked.

"Yes. I've had the bad luck of getting a string of bosses that are total egomaniacs. Totally selfish and cruel."

I decided to throw a shot in the dark.

"Ferdie, tell me about your father."

"My father? He's OK."

"Were you close?"

"No. But we're good...."

Three minutes into the conversation, my guess hit pay dirt. He shared details about his relationship with his father that were the root of his problem. His father was a self-centered person who verbally abused him almost every day as he was growing up. The man screamed at him and cursed him from head to foot — almost daily.

I realized that Ferdie had a problem with all authority figures because he had a problem with his own father. He was projecting his unresolved anger towards his bosses, making him act out in rebellion, and losing his job one after another.

"Those objects that you call poison in your house are nothing compared to the poison in your heart," I said. "Unless you remove the poison in your heart, your financial life will never change."

He neither got my point nor was he even listening. He said, "Perhaps there are still other stuff in my house that's evil. Someone gave me this odd-looking mask from Thailand. Do you think that's of the devil, too?"

Why was he insisting on removing these objects?[1]

Because it's so much easier to get rid of the physical objects than resolving his conflict with his father, healing his inner wounds and getting rid of resentments in his soul.

Because bottom line, it's easier to blame the devil than acknowledging our responsibility to change our lives.

Ferdie's financial life wasn't being destroyed by the devil. The devil didn't have to. Ferdie was destroying his own financial life by not facing the "demons" in his past. If only he'd deal with his anger towards his father, then he'd be able to respect his future boss and keep his job longer.

Stop blaming the devil for your poverty.

> Truly Rich Principle:
> **It's easier to blame the devil than to acknowledge our responsibility to change our lives.**

---

[1] I'm not saying that we shouldn't rid our homes of objects that we find contrary to our faith. That's really up to your faith. But sometimes, this becomes an escape, a distraction, to the real solution.

CHAPTER 5

Stop Blaming God for Your Poverty

If there is no wind, row.
— Latin Proverb

Some poor people believe God made them poor.

This is a deadly belief. Because religious beliefs are so deep, they become part of our core identity. And they're very difficult to dislodge.

I've heard this cruel belief spoken in various ways…

"Fate made me this way."

"If I were rich, perhaps I won't be as close to God as I am right now."

"My poverty is God's will for my life."

Whenever I hear these lines, I get angry.

This is not the God we worship!

But God gets blamed for everything.

One day, two women were talking about their diets…

Dieter #1: "Last night, I wanted to eat ice cream after work."

Dieter #2: "You didn't, right?"

Dieter #1: "Well, I asked God that if He wanted me to eat ice cream, He should give me a sign. I asked that He provide an empty parking space in front of the ice cream parlor. You know how busy that place is…"

Dieter #2: "And what happened?"

Dieter #1: "There was an empty parking space! And I ate to my heart's content."

Dieter #2: "Wow."

Dieter #1: "It was God's will. Of course, I had to go around the block seven times to find that empty parking space…."

And guess what? This same woman will blame God for her obesity.

And with the same insane logic, people will blame God for their poverty.

Later in the book, I'll explain how some people crave for poverty the way the dieter above craved for ice cream. And these poor people will look for that empty parking spot as God's sign He wants them poor — even if they have to go around the block seven times. More on this later...

Before I end, let me talk about lotto.

My friend Rex Mendoza says that Filipinos who buy lotto tickets think of it as an investment. They buy each week, usually betting one specific combination of numbers, spending huge amounts of money over the long haul. All in the hope that, one day, they'll reap their investment returns. Not realizing that their chances of winning the lotto is as rare as being hit by lightning twice in the same spot! (If only they placed their bets in an investment fund I'll talk about later in this book, their winning would have been sure.)

But here's the clincher: Many of these people actually pray to God that they win. And when they don't, they can safely blame God for keeping them poor.

Absolutely insane.

Stop blaming God.

Truly Rich Principle:
The chances of winning the lotto is equal to the likelihood of being hit by lightning twice at the same spot.

CHAPTER 6

You're the Product of Your Thoughts, Choices and Habits

If you don't like something, change it.
If you can't change it, change your attitude.
Don't complain.
— Maya Angelou

You create your life.

When you choose your thoughts, you choose your psychology.

And when you choose your psychology, you choose your behavior.

And when you choose your behavior, you choose the consequences of that behavior. Which includes wealth, or poverty.

Bottomline, you create your wealth, and you create your poverty.

We do it.

So let me ask you: What kind of thoughts do you have?

Your thoughts have power.

They have power over your body.

They have power over your abilities.

They have power over your life.

What kind of choices have you made in your life?

Some of you might be saying right now, "OK, Bo. I'm going to create my own life starting now."

You got me wrong. You don't get it. This is an absolute law. You've been creating your life a long, long time ago. Even if you didn't know you were doing it. By the choices that you made in the past (even the choice of not choosing), you were creating your life.

You are where you are right now because of the choices you've made.

Excellence is not an act but a habit. We are what we repeatedly do.
— Aristotle

You become what you repeatedly do.

Do you pray daily? You become a prayerful person.

Do you choose to be positive every day? You become a positive person.

Do you grumble, complain and criticize every day? You become a negative person.

Do you postpone, delay, become lazy daily? You become a bum.

Failure is not a single, cataclysmic event. You don't fail overnight. Instead, failure is a few errors in judgment, repeated every day.
— Jim Rohn

For example, you don't get overweight overnight. You don't eat a blueberry cheesecake tonight and get obese tomorrow. You get overweight by living a sedentary life coupled with a lot of blueberry cheesecakes over a period of time.

In the same way, poverty doesn't happen overnight. You become poor because you have the poor man's money habits. You have bad debts. You don't save. You spend beyond your means. You don't study how money works.

Failure usually happens not in one dramatic event. Failure happens bit by bit, one negative act after another negative act, done consistently over time.

You're the product of your thoughts, choices and habits.

Truly Rich Principle:
You become what you repeatedly do. You become poor because you have the poor man's money habits.

CHAPTER 7

You Can Create a New Pattern of Success

Man is not the creature of circumstances;
Circumstances are the creatures of men.
— Benjamin Disraeli

Let me tell you my story.

When I was growing up, I felt I was the most ungifted kid in the entire world.

Honest! I had four things going against me.

First, my grades were bad.

As early as Grade 2, I failed in Math and Pilipino — two subjects I abhorred like *ampalaya*[1] juice concentrate or an antibiotic capsule that accidentally breaks open on your tongue. Yuck.

I felt I was dumb exponentially raised to the power of three. My academic goal in life was to reach the high grade of 75. One day, one of my subjects reached 82 and I almost collapsed in shock. I went to my teacher and asked if she made a mistake.

Today, I'm guessing I probably had some form of mild dyslexia, but during my time, they just called it *bobo.*[2]

Second, I was bad in sports.

Some kids were dumb but at least they were good in sports.

But I was *bano.*[3]

I dreaded P.E.[4] It was pure social torture.

For example, the teacher would ask me to dribble the ball — and while everyone would watch — I'd lose the ball, chase after it, manage to step on it, slip and splatter myself on the floor. And everyone would burst out laughing for five minutes straight. Yep, even the teacher would laugh. (Do you notice my deep resentments coming out here?)

---

[1] bitter gourd
[2] stupid
[3] physically uncoordinated
[4] Physical Education

Obviously, no team wanted me. I was left standing alone until the teacher forced one of the teams to get me. So I'd enter the game and make them lose 10 points in 10 seconds. (I did the impossible.) And they'd hate me to bits.

Third, I was poor.

My allowance was 50 centavos a day when the prevailing rate was two pesos.

I remember going to the canteen clutching my 50 centavos in my hand. "Coke please," I asked. The saleslady looked at my coin and said, "Coke is 60." I looked at the other goodies and asked again, "Cheeze Curls please." She shook her head, "That's 60, too." I finally asked, "What can I buy with 50 centavos?" She looked around and fished out something tiny. "Marie,"[5] she said.

At that precise moment, my classmate stood beside me with a five-peso bill and said, "Coke, Cheese Curls and a hotdog sandwich please."

Triple ouch.

Fourth, I was ugly.

Yes I *was.* (I know it's hard to imagine that now...)

They called me refugee and *tipaklong.*[6]

Let me say this again: I felt I was the most ungifted person God ever created.

But today, I write books, compose songs, publish magazines, produce concerts, lead organizations, speak on radio and TV, run small businesses... just to name a few things I do today.

I didn't become Albert Einstein but I literally changed my life.

Speaking of Albert Einstein, did you know he was dumb in school?

Here are three actual quotes from his school teachers:

No matter what you do, you will never amount to anything.

— Albert Einstein's first teacher

Your mere presence spoils the respect of the class for me.

— Albert Einstein's second teacher

---

[5] a biscuit

[6] grasshopper

It doesn't matter; he'll never make a success of anything.

— The response of Albert Einstein's teacher to his father's question on what profession Einstein should pursue.

They were almost right. Because at age 16, Albert Einstein failed an entrance exam to a polytechnic college in Zurich.

What happened to that dumb kid? Why did he come to be one of the greatest scientists of the world?

You can create a new pattern of success.

SECRET 2

Enlarge Your Psychological Wallet

There is a secret psychology to money. Most people don't know about it. That's why most people never become financially successful.
A lack of money is not the problem; it is merely a symptom of what's going on inside you.
— T. Harv Eker

The first giant reason why people are poor is because they *don't* want to be rich.

As absurd as this may sound, it's true.

Because subconsciously, we don't think it fits us. We feel it's not who we are.

Here's what I learned.

If you want to make small incremental improvements in your life, change your behavior. But if you want to make dramatic, quantum leaps in your life, change your beliefs.

So many people are trying to change their *behavior.*

They try to save.

They study how to invest.

They start a tiny business.

But it's not enough unless they rewire their thinking process. Otherwise the old thinking will sabotage their new behavior.

Let me repeat what I said in the first page of this book.

Your money problems are mind problems.

And the first mind problem *is your core beliefs about yourself.*

Unless you change your picture of yourself in your mind, it will be almost impossible to get rich. Even if you have all the skills and connections in the world. Even if you earn huge amounts of money, you'll lose it all again — if you don't enlarge your psychological wallet.

Tony Meloto, founder of Gawad Kalinga — an amazing movement that builds homes and rebuilds lives of the poorest of the poor — says, "I've realized that poverty isn't the lack of jobs or the lack of money. It's the lack of dignity. The poor have lost their ability to dream. That's why we build very colorful GK houses. When the new owner of a GK house wakes up each morning and sees the bright colors of his home, he realizes that he can dream again."

Enlarge your psychological wallet.

CHAPTER 8

Face Your Feelings

What you can feel, you can heal.
— John Gray

The poor have tiny psychological wallets.

God wants to give them more but their psychology can't handle the blessing.

Let me give you an example in my life.

Last month, I earned more money than I ever earned in any single month of my entire life. (Of course, the phrase "more money" is a relative term. What may be a lot of money to me may be loose change to some of you.)

But because it was "too much" for me — way beyond what I was accustomed to — I actually felt very uncomfortable. In other words, the money didn't fit my psychological wallet. The money didn't match my perceived identity.

I sat with these raw feelings for a while, and identified them as fear and guilt.

I was afraid because it was a new experience of earning that huge amount of money.

And I felt guilty because I may be doing something wrong.

With a stern schoolteacher's voice, I "heard" these loud thoughts within:

You should be ashamed of yourself. You earn more in one month what some poor people earn in years. How could you be so unfair?

You should be ashamed of yourself. You're no longer doing God's will. You're so focused on money now.

You should be ashamed of yourself. If you're going to heaven, why waste your time and be busy with material things?

They were powerful emotions and I had to face them.

Or they would be like ticking time bombs, ready to explode at a later time, and destroy whatever financial progress I have attained.

I needed to learn how to face these raw emotions and deal with them.

Thankfully, through the years, I've learned to feel them, embrace them and bring them to God.

Were they telling me the truth? Then I should obey the truth.

Or were they telling me lies? Then I should reject them.

Or were they telling me half-truths and half-lies? Then I need to pick the grain of truth in them and obey that truth, but in the same breath, toss away the lies so as not to contaminate the truth.

After allowing myself to feel and identify these disruptive feelings, I asked myself: Why am I earning money? Why am I in business anyway?

I searched deep in my heart and found two simple answers:

First, because I love my family.

I'm not a celibate priest but a husband and father of two kids. I need to earn money or I wouldn't be doing God's will.

Second, because I want to love beyond my family.

I'm not content with earning "enough." My heart is too big just for my own family. I want to earn "more than enough" so that I could bless the poor and the ministries of God.

Slowly, the disturbing emotions became calm.

I searched my heart for the shadow of greed.

Was money really becoming my lord?

Did I trust wealth more than God now?

My answer was no.

But these were beautiful questions — and I promised God that I'd always ask myself these questions before His Presence.

And like night giving way to the breaking of dawn, the feelings of false guilt and fear faded in the light of truth.

I learned this from best-selling author John Gray: "We cannot heal what we do not feel." Because I allowed myself to feel these dark emotions before God's discerning Presence, I removed their urgency. In one sense, I defanged them. I removed their poison. Knowledge is power, and knowing that they were there within me made me their superior.

What would have happened if I didn't do this?

Then these dark emotions would creep up from my subconscious, and I'd start sabotaging my financial success. I've seen this happen to so many people. They'll make one bad decision after another. Or they'll get sick. Or they'll simply lose interest in their business until it collapses.

Face your feelings.

> Truly Rich Principle:
> **I'm not content with earning "enough." My heart is too big for that. I want to earn "more than enough" so I could bless the poor.**

CHAPTER 9

Increase Your Money Comfort Zone

You are the way you are because that's the way you want to be.
If you really wanted to be any different,
you would be in the process of changing right now.
— Fred Smith

I had to enlarge my psychological wallet.

Some call it our money comfort zone.

Can you imagine yourself with a million?

Some can't even picture this scene. Some can picture it but they immediately feel uncomfortable. As though there's something wrong with the picture.

For example, some have a P10,000 psychological wallet.

They see themselves earning P10,000 a month — nothing less, nothing more.

If, for example, they get a bonus of P20,000, they'll be happy on the outside, but subconsciously, they're panicking on the inside.

And so they'll force themselves to lose it all (usually by spending it) so that they can go back to their comfortable P10,000 identity.

They'll buy the dress, the shoes, the cell phone.

Anything just to get rid of the money.

Just so that they can get back to their financial bondage.

A study was made involving lotto winners who've won millions of dollars. A huge percentage of these winners lose it all after a few years. In five years' time, they find themselves in the exact same financial condition they were in before they won.

Why?

Because the millions couldn't fit their psychological wallet. Something in them rebelled. So they "got rid" of it.

Some have a P30,000 psychological wallet.

Some have a P50,000, a P100,000 and a P500,000 a month psychological wallet.

What's yours?

How much money are you comfortable with?

If you want to get rich, the first thing you need to do is to enlarge your psychological wallet.

Increase your money comfort zone.

CHAPTER 10

Unless You See It in Your Mind, It Won't Become Reality

It's time to start living the life you've imagined.
— Henry James

Deep within you, you've programmed your life to operate on a particular level of income and total net worth. Because this is your psychological wallet or money comfort zone, you can't see yourself earning twice as much or becoming a millionaire. You simply can't. Something within you says, "Are you nuts? Me? Earn twice as much? Become a millionaire? Hah! I might as well imagine I'm Donald Duck."

So you stay in your money comfort zone for the rest of your life.

It affects your love life, too.

More likely, you'll subconsciously get attracted to marry someone who also has the same size as your psychological wallet. So both of you can comfortably live in that zone happily ever after.

Well, I've got news for you.

Do you know who set that dial of your inner financial thermostat?

You did.

So anytime you like, you, too, can enlarge your psychological wallet to any size you want. You can raise your money comfort zone.

How? Start with your imagination.

Imagine yourself earning double of what you're earning now by next year—through wise investing and some side business.

That's right. Double.

Get comfortable with that.

See yourself not spending it all, but actually saving it, learning how to invest it and seeing your money grow.

See yourself with a business on the side, aside from your full-time job.

See yourself as an investor.

See yourself giving generously — writing large checks — addressed to Bo Sanchez for his projects for the poor and his media ministry. (As you can see, this book has ulterior motives.)

You've got to see it in your mind.

Each week, Bro. Mike Velarde preaches to 300,000 people in the El Shaddai prayer meeting. That figure boggles my mind. During their anniversary, a million people congregated at the Luneta Grandstand. It was the late Jaime Cardinal Sin who asked him, "Bro. Mike, what do you have that I don't have? Why do these people come when you call them to come?"

One day, I had a three-hour chat with Bro. Mike Velarde to ask him why.

"The grace of God," he said over and over again.

I believe him. Last Christmas, he invited me to preach to his massive audience — and I saw it before my eyes. Three hundred thousand people receiving grace!

And Bro. Mike does it by giving them hope. That's why they keep coming back.

Bro. Mike asks them to raise their wallets for financial blessings — and 300,000 wallets go up.

He asks those who want to migrate to other countries to raise their passports — and thousands of green booklets are up in the air.

He makes them *imagine* their answered prayer. That they are healed. That they are debt-free. That they are working abroad.

In a very simple way, he makes them set goals and aim for them by the power of their imagination, by the power of their faith.

Unless you see it in your mind, it won't become reality.

Truly Rich Principle:
See yourself earning double of what you're earning now. Get comfortable with that.

CHAPTER 11

Your Self-Image Will Attract Your Level of Success

People do not attract that which they want,
but that which they are.
– James Allen

James Allen is right.

But let me go one step further. It should be written this way: "People do not attract that which they want, but that which they think they are."

Your picture of yourself isn't just a picture. It's a photograph of the future.

This works in non-financial aspects of your life, too.

For example, if you can't see yourself as a "fantastic father to my children," then you won't be spending time with your kids on a daily basis, building your relationship with them. You won't do that because it's not who you think you are.

Remember this truth. At the end of the day, who you are doesn't count.

It's who you *think* you are that determines your success.

Because you'll be acting according to that picture.

Here's the suggestion from the preacher in me: Ask God who He thinks you are. And you'll be amazed at the dazzling picture He has of you. You'll be blown away by how much He believes in you.

Get a new picture of who you are by actually working on yourself.

This is the secret that unlocks all success. Dennis Waitley says, "When you stop working on what it is you're trying to get, and start working on YOU, only then will you get what it is you want."

Your self-image will attract your level of success.

> Truly Rich Principle:
> **At the end of the day, who you are doesn't count.**
> **It's who you *think* you are that determines**
> **your success.**

CHAPTER 12

Are You Sending Mixed Signals to God's Universe?

What you subconsciously want, you will get.
And what you subconsciously do not want, you will avoid.
— Bo Sanchez

I've long learned that God's universe simply responds to what we want — clearly, repeatedly and passionately.

You can gain all the financial wisdom in the world, but unless you sort out your unconscious wrong beliefs about money or negative image of yourself in relation to money, you'll be sending up confused, muddled, incoherent messages to God's universe.

Let me tell you why.

Many people are trapped in poverty specifically because of their mixed-up, conflicting desires: On one hand, they want to get rich, pay their debts and be generous. On the other hand, in a very deep unconscious level, they don't want to get rich.

Shocking?

Because of their subconscious beliefs that money is bad, that rich people are evil, and that business is dirty, they'll actually avoid wealth. Some of these beliefs are distorted religious beliefs — but religious, nonetheless. And religious beliefs are very, very deeply rooted within our spirit. They are part of our core identity. (We'll talk more about this in Secret #3.)

So how could these people ever prosper?

They're sending out mixed messages to themselves, to their bodies, to their emotions, to their jobs, to their bosses, to their customers and to the universe.

Contradicting desires create contradicting results.

Where there is no clarity of purpose, no great thing will be achieved.

So what do you really want?

Are you sending mixed signals to God's universe?

Truly Rich Principle:
Contradicting desires create contradicting results.

CHAPTER 13

Rip Out Your Negative Family Labels

Men and women are not limited by the place of their birth, not by the color of their skin, but by the size of their hope.
— John Johnson

Some parents "train" their kids to have very small psychological wallets.

We inherit the size of our psychological wallets from our families.

I hear this dialogue a lot in toy stores:

Junior: "Mommy, can you buy this toy for me?"

Mother: "No son, we can't afford that."

Junior: "But Mommy, this toy is really nice."

Mother: "Son, didn't you hear me? We're not rich!"

Junior: "But Mommy, I really, really like this toy!"

Mother: "For the last time, son, I'm going to say it again. Get this into your skull. Your family is poor! Your mother is poor! You are poor!"

The child grows up with that label tattooed in his brain: "I'm poor."

Unless he tears out this family label knitted into his psychology, he will always act like a poor person.

Can I suggest another kind of dialogue?

Junior: "Mommy, can you buy this toy?"

Mother: "We can buy that but we're choosing not to."

Junior: "But Mommy, this toy is really nice."

Mother: "Son, we can afford it and can buy it right now. But because we're financially wise people, we'd rather invest our money so that it keeps on growing."

Rip out your negative family labels.

Truly Rich Principle:
You inherit the size of your psychological wallet from your family. If it's too small, get a bigger one.

CHAPTER 14

Train Them While They're Young

The greatest gifts you can give your children are the roots of responsibility and the wings of independence.
— Dennis Waitely

One day, when my son was five years old, he wanted to buy a toy—a Power Rangers robot.

"Will you buy this for me, Daddy?" he asked.

I shook my head. "You need to earn money to buy that."

"How?"

"Set up a business," I told him. "What can you sell?"

His face lit up. "I'll sell *bangus!*" (milkfish).

My fellow leader and friend, Pio Español, sells Bonuan Bangus as his business — and our whole family loves it.

So I told Bene, "Go for it. I'll tell *Tito* Pio to make you one of his dealers."

When we got home, my son got a piece of paper and made a "prospect" list — people who would buy his *bangus.* I saw him writing, "*Lola* Linda, *Ninong* Robee, Cousin Denise..." and seven other names of family members.

Meanwhile, I typed up a list of the *bangus* products and printed a leaflet.

Bene grabbed a yellow necktie, wore it over his sando and shorts, and scooted out the door — with leaflet in hand. He rode his little three-wheel bike to his *Lola's* house, gave the leaflet to her, and said, "Just call anytime!"

For the next few days, my son kept giving his leaflets away.

In the first week, he sold P3,000 worth of *bangus.*

Let me remind you how old my son was: five years old.

He also told me he's giving a tithe to the Lord and share with the poor.

I don't know how long his *bangus* business will last.

But this I know: The lessons he's learning will last a lifetime. He's learning that it's OK to have lots of money (Lesson #1). He's learning that in the real world, you don't get toys for free (Lesson #2). You earn it. You work for it. He's also learning that it's *easy* to earn money if you focus on it (Lesson #3). (This is shocking to some people. More on this later.) He's also learning that earning profits is better than earning a salary (Lesson #4). For example, I've never paid him for chores. I'm programming him to have an entrepreneur's mindset. And he's learning that there's no shame in selling — that it's a fantastic way to serve (Lesson #5).

Yesterday, Bene told me, "I want to sell another product." (How many of you know of other five-year-olds who use the word "product"?)

I asked, "What son?"

"My music CD," he smiled, "I'll sing my songs."

From *bangus* dealer to rock star.

To a five-year-old, almost everything is possible if you believe.

Gosh. We need to learn that lesson again.

Train them while they're young.

Truly Rich Principle:
There's no shame in selling. It's a fantastic way to serve.

CHAPTER 15

Enlarge Your Skills to Match the Size of Your Psychological Wallet

Do you see a man skilled in his work?
He will serve before kings; he will not serve before obscure men.
— Proverbs 22:29

My son believes he's rich.

So when he sees someone in need, he says, "I have money. Let's give him money." His psychological wallet is big.

For a long time, we were praying for a friend's baby who needed a liver transplant. My friend needed P3 million for the surgery.

After our usual evening prayers, my son asked me, "Daddy, why don't you give P3 million to that baby?"

I almost choked. "Because I don't have P3 million."

And then it hit me: What's stopping me from earning P3 million a month?

Only two things: My beliefs and my skills.

First, I don't see myself earning P3 million a month. I can't imagine it.

And what I cannot see in my mind will never happen in reality.

But the moment my heart believes it can happen, then it becomes possible.

But here's the other factor: I also don't have the level of skill necessary to earn P3 million a month.

And so that's what I'm trying to do now.

I'm learning from various mentors and filling the gaps in my skill level.

So now, I'm learning more about marketing, from direct marketing to Internet marketing, from copywriting to selling, etc.

I'm also learning more about investing in stocks — here and abroad.

And I'm learning how to run more complex operations.

I've already enlarged my psychological wallet.

Now, I need to enlarge my skills to match the size of my psychological wallet.

Do the same. Ask yourself and ask your mentors: What skills do I need?

We'll discuss more about these skills in Secret 6: *Ride Something to Wealth.*

Enlarge your skills to match the size of your psychological wallet.

SECRET 3

Get Rid of Crazy Religious Beliefs

The mind maketh good or ill, wretch or happy, rich or poor.
— Edmund Spenser

You may be wondering what in the world "Religious Beliefs" are doing here in a book about money.

Answer: Your religious beliefs determine your wealth more than you think.

Let me say it again. One of the biggest monsters that keep us poor is that we really don't want to be rich. And we don't want to be rich because we've got crazy, insane religious beliefs about money.

Religious beliefs are so deep, so wedged to your core identity, you follow them even if you're not aware that you're following them.

In this book, I'm NOT in any way insinuating that all people should try to be rich, yada, yada, yada. Or that we're defined by how much we earn. Mother Teresa had zero income but she's one of the greatest persons this century has ever had.

But because of her work for the poorest of the poor, she spent $40 million a year. Her ministry was blessed by very rich people helping her. How could she have done her incredible work if there were no generous people around her?

Friends, I'm against the idea that people who do want to become rich are automatically judged as spiritually immature and in need of deliverance from the evil spirits.

It's all a matter of purpose.

Read carefully...

Money isn't the most important thing in the world.

But money affects every important thing in the world.

It affects your family life.

It affects your physical life.

It affects your intellectual life.

It affects your spiritual life.

It affects your ability to help others.

We need money. And money, if used properly, can bless the world.

Get rid of crazy religious beliefs.

CHAPTER 16

Have You Romanticized Poverty?

Blessed are the poor.
— Luke 6:20

Religion can romanticize poverty.

We can receive this message: "To be poor is better than to be rich. It's more pleasing to God. He favors the poor. Poor people go to heaven. Rich people go to hell."

If you believe in this philosophy, then goodness, why in the world would anyone even think of becoming rich?

Yes, it's true that God favors the poor. And it's true that the Bible says, "Blessed are the poor" (Luke 6:20). But I believe God loves the poor and accompanies them in their difficult journey *so that they can rise from their poverty.* Not so that they can remain in their poverty!

It's foolish to romanticize poverty.

Whoever says being poor is romantic is out of his mind.

When I was 15 years old, I lived and ministered in the slums — and I'm telling you, there's nothing romantic about it.

I lived in a house with nine other people. And we all slept in one single room that's about the size of your office cubicle.

We also shared the same dark, damp, muddy toilet with four other families. (Can you imagine how interesting my mornings were lining up for it?) I ate their food and lived their life.

The entire area was flooded nine months of the year. Stagnant water reached my knees. I remember seeing an entire army of mosquitoes living, eating, partying, laughing, making love and hatching millions of eggs around us. It may have been romantic for the mosquitoes but it wasn't romantic for us.

And there's nothing romantic about the baby I heard crying in the middle of the night because her mother had no money to buy milk.

There's nothing romantic about the old man I met next door who needed a doctor because of severe pneumonia, but his family couldn't even pay for the jeepney fare to the hospital.

There's nothing romantic about the almost weekly stabbings in the street because of rampant drug addiction.

Poverty is evil. Period!

And God wants us to get rid of it.

You also need to get rid of it in your life — so that you can get rid of it in the lives of others. If you want the Philippines to become a first world country, become a first world citizen first.

Have you romanticized poverty?

Truly Rich Principle:
You need to get rid of poverty from your life so that you can get rid of it in the lives of others.

CHAPTER 17

Do You Believe That the Rich Won't Enter Heaven?

Again, I tell you, it is easier for a camel to go through the eye of a needle than for a rich man to enter the kingdom of God.
— Matthew 19:24

The verse above is often quoted as proof that heaven isn't for rich people.

I've got two problems with that.

First of all, they don't read the two verses right after that verse...

> *When the disciples heard this, they were greatly astonished and asked, "Who then can be saved? Jesus looked at them and said, "With man this is impossible, but with God all things are possible.*
> — Matthew 19:25-26

Jesus didn't say, "It's impossible for rich people to enter heaven." He simply said, "It's going to be more difficult for the rich person to enter heaven." Why is this? Because Jesus says that to whom much is given, much more will be required (Luke 12:48).

Anyone who has more talents, for example, will also be judged in a different way than one who has less. Paul even says, "Not many of you should presume to be teachers, my brothers, because you know that we who teach will be judged more strictly" (James 3:1).

If you're a teacher, that means it's also more difficult to enter heaven.

So should I be terrified of severe judgment and give up preaching? Oh woe is me, what have I done? I preach 300 times a year. My goodness. Should I resign today and find myself another job? (Hmm. I wonder if I can be a male ramp model....)

Wait a minute. Who then will preach if everyone says, "Don't be a preacher. It's so difficult to go to heaven because on Judgment Day, you'll be judged more strictly."

This is silly thinking.

In the same way, don't avoid wealth simply because it's difficult to enter heaven.

Because God needs godly people who will run businesses, give jobs, and bless the world with great services and great products.

Here's my second point: Don't take the "camel through an eye of a needle" literally. The illustration is so out-of-this-world, no wonder people think it's impossible.

But when Jesus said, "camel through an eye of a needle," ancient Jews would have immediately understood what He was referring to. "The eye of a needle" was a common idiom for the doorway of a camel's home.

The doorway is very small. So a camel coming home from a very rich caravan should do two things to enter into it. First, he needs to unload his bags from his back. Second, he has to stoop down and crawl inside.

And thus we get the meaning of this passage: We now know what a rich person needs to do. First, he needs to unload his wealth either by literally giving it all away (as celibates in religious congregations do), or by spiritually detaching himself from all his wealth as all of us should do.

Second, he should stoop down before God and acknowledge that all belongs to Him. A rich person must remain humble before the Lord and before others.

What if Tony Tan of Jollibee responded to this particular Bible passage by saying, "Gosh, rich people can't enter heaven? I won't go into business...."

Then, thousands upon thousands of people won't have jobs today. I know because each year, my own Beaconlight Corporate Training Team gives powerful leadership and life-management seminars to over a thousand Jollibee store managers (who love their jobs, by the way.) Where would they be if Tony decided not to get into business?

Thank God, his response was very different.

Remember: The rich can go to heaven if they're truly rich.

It's not impossible, only more difficult.

Don't be afraid of a challenge.

Do you believe that the rich won't enter heaven?

Truly Rich Principle:
God needs godly people who will run businesses, give jobs, and bless the world with great services and great products.

CHAPTER 18

Do You Practice the "I Hate Myself" Spirituality?

Love your neighbor as you love yourself.
— Matthew 22:39

Some strains of religion encourage self-hatred.

In some religious circles, if you don't like yourself, you're considered a saint.

That's a lot of chicken poop but a lot of people believe in it.

If someone says, "Oh, woe is me. I'm the most rotten, most miserable, most evil, most depraved man on the face of the earth, and I hate me! I hate me! I hate me!" some people will actually canonize him on the spot as a saint.

Friends, that's no saint.

That guy needs therapy. Quick.

He's sick. He's got low self – worth and self-pity all over him.

Here's my belief. Unless you love yourself, you can't love anyone else.

This low self-worth trip spills over their financial life.

Because they believe they deserve rubbish, that's what they'll get. They'll remain poor because they believe that's their punishment for the sins they committed.

And worse, they'll be locked into that poverty because they believe God is pleased that they're suffering! And they look "down" at rich people as being materialistic and going to hell.

Hogwash.

Let me assume you're a good, decent, normal parent. (You're not a psycho who eats your children when they reach seven years old.)

Do you want your children to suffer?

No. You suffer when they suffer. Much more than they do, right?

God is no different.

When He sees us suffering in poverty, He weeps.

He wants the best for us.

That's why I suspect that the god many people worship is psycho. Because their god takes delight in the fact that his kids suffer.

Let me shout this from the housetops: Poverty isn't His will for 99.99 percent of His children. Who's the 0.01 percent? Religious celibates and missionaries called to that special life. The great scandal of the past 2,000 years is that this life of poverty for this special group of people comprising 0.01 percent has been imposed as the great model for the other 99.99 percent.

And what untold suffering this has caused!

Married lay people need another model.

And this is what this book is all about.

Do you practice the "I Hate Myself" spirituality?

Truly Rich Principle:
Some people remain poor because they believe they're being punished, that it's the will of God. Hogwash. When God sees us in poverty, He weeps.

CHAPTER 19

Have You Relied on God Too Much?

Trust God, but tie your camel.
— Old Persian proverb

Many years ago, when I was still young and handsome (now I'm just handsome), I was giving a retreat to a bunch of college women.

While preparing for my talks in my bedroom, a regular sized cockroach flew in and buzzed around the ceiling. I didn't know why I did this, but I found myself pointing my finger to it and commanded, "In Jesus' name, come down and die!"

In a second, I saw the insect hit an invisible wall and come crashing down on the hard floor, dead as a stone.

Suddenly, I felt powerful. I lifted my pointer finger to my lips and blew the imaginary smoke.

A few minutes later, I was preaching to an enthusiastic crowd of young female college students. Without warning, a bigger cockroach came into the seminar room — probably the grandfather of the critter I killed, seeking vengeance.

You can just imagine the dramatic effect this had on an all-women audience. They were busy ducking for shelter and hiding beneath desks. My talk was losing much of its appeal.

I remembered what I did in my room a few minutes ago, so I pointed my finger to the flying beast and ordered, "In Jesus' name, come down and die!"

And the same thing happened: The flyer nose dived and splattered its entrails on the cement tiles in front of me.

Naturally, my audience was shocked. As if this was an everyday occurrence for me, I casually said, "As I was saying...."

After my talk, I went back to my bedroom. That was when I saw another cockroach climbing the bedroom wall. (Out of the kindness of my heart, I shall not divulge the name of this retreat house.) So with my two recent "power" encounters, I knew what to do. I pointed my finger to it and said, "In Jesus' name, come down and die!"

But this time, the crawler kept going.

Thinking that perhaps it didn't have his antennas up, I repeated my command in a louder voice. But the cockroach didn't show any signs of obeying me.

Suddenly, a clear inspiration from God entered my mind. He said, *"Kunin mo yung tsinelas mo at patayin mo! Tamad!"* [1] And then I heard God laugh. And I ended up laughing on the floor, too.

But I have a serious message in my story.

I believe that one of the biggest reasons why we don't receive God's blessings is because we rely on Him too much. We surrender to Him what He *doesn't* want us to surrender: **our stewardship.**

Have you relied on God too much?

Truly Rich Principle:
Don't expect God to do the very things He expects you to do.

[1] Get your slippers and kill it, lazy guy!

CHAPTER 20

Do You Disguise Your Laziness as Faith?

Lazy hands make a man poor, but diligent hands bring wealth.
— Proverbs 10:4

Are you expecting God to do the very things He expects you to do?

This is a true story.

One day, Bernie asked me to pray that he gets a nice job. "I know He will give me the best job," he said happily.

A few months later, I saw Bernie in a prayer meeting depressed. "God didn't answer my prayer," he complained, "Why didn't He bless me with a job?"

I patted him on the back and asked, "How many companies did you apply for?"

His answer jolted me. "One," he said with a pout.

"One?" I asked, "For crying out loud, Bernie, you sent your resumé to one measly company?"

"Yeah. Why?"

"And you have the gall to complain to God that He didn't bless your job hunt? Bernie, start complaining after sending out *one hundred* job applications! Not *one*!"

Many of us are like Bernie.

We want God to give us everything on a silver platter. No sweat. No effort. No tears. No struggle. Just because we prayed.

But most times, that's not how God operates. Because He usually uses the sweat, the effort, the tears and the struggle to form our character.

Don't confuse faith with your laziness.

Faith requires action.

James 2:17 says, "In the same way, faith by itself, if it is not accompanied by action, is dead."

Do you disguise your laziness as faith?

Truly Rich Principle:
God usually uses the sweat, the effort, the tears and the struggle you go through to form your character.

CHAPTER 21

Are You Obsessed with the Purely Miraculous?

Make it your ambition to lead a quiet life, to mind your own business and to work with your hands... so that you will not be dependent on anybody.
— 1 Thessalonians 4:11-12

Let me give you a parable.

Letty, a plumpish woman with a red bandana on her head, stands up in a prayer meeting and shares, "For a long time, I've asked God to solve my financial problems." She gets a hankie and wipes her tears. "I've been buried in debt for years! But recently, I started a bananacue[1] stand." At this point, she begins to smile. "Brothers and sisters, I praise God because in six months, I was able to pay all my debts! God is good!"

Everybody applauds and rejoices with Letty.

Sonia takes the microphone. A more slender woman with large eyeglasses, she says, "I, too, had the same problems like Letty. I had loans left and right. I wanted to commit suicide." She also gets a hankie and blows her nose. "I asked God to help me, and one day, I bought a lotto ticket. I went to church and asked the Lord that it be the winning ticket. Brothers and sisters, the next day, I found out that I won one million pesos! Praise the Lord!"

Do you think people will applaud louder for the second sharing?

You can bet your life on it.

But I don't agree with the louder applause. I'm not saying Sonia's miracle didn't come from God. But I'm going to applaud louder for Letty and her bananacue. I'll even give her a standing ovation. Why?

Letty has learned to be God's steward.

[1] A common snack in the Philippines: Fried banana with brown sugar

She worked in her bananacue business, and her inner character was formed, her perseverance increased, her industry multiplied.

Because if Sonia won't be able to learn these same things, you can be sure that she'll be back to her financial problems in a few years — after her million has run out.

Sure, Letty's story isn't as dramatic as Sonia's. Nor is it "purely" miraculous.

But in my book, Letty's story is the bigger miracle, because holiness and obedience to God is always the bigger miracle.

Are you obsessed with the purely miraculous?

CHAPTER 22

Is Your Favorite Phrase "*Bahala Na*"?[1]

...if any would not work, neither should he eat.
— 2 Thessalonians 3:10

This Filipino trait is the source of many of our problems.

We rely on fate. We accept things and try to live with whatever crazy circumstances befall us. But many times, God is calling us to *change* the situation.

But unfortunately, saying *"Bahala na!"* is easier than changing things.

An overweight man is eating two kilos of *lechon*[2] and *chicharon bulaklak.*[3] When friends caution him to slow down, he says, *"Masarap eh.*[4] *Bahala na."*

An overloaded ship is heavy with excess passengers. When some ask whether this is dangerous, the crew will say, *"Eh, gustong sumakay ang mga tao.*[5] *Bahala na."*

But this is insane. God wants us to be good stewards.

Bahala na can be our strength if we do one thing: We should first be good stewards and then rely on God. *Bahala na* is actually rooted in our local word for God: *Bathala*. What we're saying is that we're turning the situation over to God. And that's very good. **But not before we do what we're supposed to do.**

My message: *God designed us to work and trust — not simply to trust.*

So develop your skills as your expression of loving God!

[1] "What will be, will be."
[2] Roasted pig
[3] Deep fried pig's intestines
[4] It's delicious!
[5] Passengers want to ride.

Be a better human being and you glorify the One who made you. Pray with me now.

God, grant me the serenity
To accept the things I cannot change,
Courage to change the things I can,
And the wisdom to know the difference.

Is your favorite phrase "*bahala na*"?

Truly Rich Principle:
God designed us to work and trust — not just to trust.

SECRET 4

Be Completely Committed to Your Dreams

If a man hasn't discovered something that he will die for, he isn't fit to live.
— Martin Luther King, Jr.

Have you ever wondered why you do not get what you want?

There are two big reasons why you fail to get what you want.

First, because you don't really know what you want. That means, you're confused with what you want. As I mentioned in the previous Secrets, many people are mixed up with what they want concerning wealth. And so they send mixed signals to the universe.

The second big reason for not getting what we want is that *we don't want it bad enough.* And this is the message of Secret #4.

There are three levels of desire. It doesn't matter what you desire. You could desire to be an Olympic gold medallist or build an orphanage for God or be a recording artist with a platinum album or earn a million. The results are always the same at each level.

The first level of desire is called the **Wish** level.

For example: "I wish I was rich."

Usually, nothing happens at the level of wish.

So many people are in this first level.

That's why people get shocked when I say that one of the reasons why we're poor is because we actually don't like to be rich.

People argue, "Bo, almost everyone I talk to wants to get rich!"

Yes, but only from a level of wish. You hear stuff like....

"It would be nice to be rich."

"Oh, to have some extra money to help others...."

"Gosh, what would it feel like to have a million in the bank?"

I repeat: Nothing much happens when you stay on this level.

The second level of desire is called the **Want** level.

In this level, people say, "I want to be rich."

OK, some things happen here.

A little action. Perhaps some smoke and spark appear.

But sadly, not for long.

A few people move up to this level, but level 2 is still not enough to bring them to the finish line.

The third level is the **Commitment** level.

In this level, people say, "I'm committed to be rich."

In this level, you believe that when you say these words, you're prophesying your future. You know it will happen.

Only very few people are in this level of desire, but *commitment* is where anything of value is created in this world.

Do you want to be truly rich?

Then be committed.

There's no other way.

Be completely committed to your dreams.

CHAPTER 23

Be the Scriptwriter of Your Life

Let others lead small lives, but not you.
Let others argue over small things, but not you.
Let others cry over small hurts, but not you.
Let others leave their future in someone else's hands, but not you.
— Jim Rohn

To help people write their dreams, I created the *Life Dreams Success Journal.*[1] In it I wrote that when it comes to self-direction, there are three kinds of people in this world.

First is the **Moviegoer.**

This person watches the movie of her life, admires some parts and criticizes other parts. Aside from that, she does nothing else. All she says the whole day is, "I like this thing but I don't like that thing." The Moviegoer feels she has absolutely no control over her life — except to comment about it. *Moviegoers are the most pathetic, miserable people in the world.*

Second is the **Actor**.

This person doesn't only watch the movie of her life. She actually realizes she's the Actor — and can control a big part of her life. She can actually make or break the movie — by how well she delivers her lines and by how she portrays her character. *Actors are a happy bunch. They realize they're the star of the show and enjoy some level of control. But many times, they wish the movie would end in another way — but realize that they have no say in such things.*

[1] You can buy any notebook or use your computer to write life dreams. You can also use my *Life Dreams Success Journal*. However, it's not being sold. I give it for FREE to all Kerygma Family members who support our ministry of sharing God's love through media and Anawim, our ministry for the poorest of the poor. Go to **www.kerygmafamily.com to sign up as a member.**

Third is the **Actor-Scriptwriter**.

This person doesn't only watch, and she doesn't only act, but she actually *creates* the entire movie from her mind. She determines what she will say, what she will do and how the movie will end. She realizes she has enormous control over her life, and sees to it that the movie of her life will turn out beautiful.

Let me ask you this question: Who are you among these three people?

Do you merely watch your life go by?

Or do you act out a script that you feel has been handed to you?

Or do you write the script and make your life beautiful?

Friend, make a decision now to become the Scriptwriter of your life.

God *wants* you to be the Scriptwriter.

Create the life you were meant to live.

By the way, you might be asking: Where is God in the movie?

He's the *Producer.*

He says, "Make the movie beautiful. Here's the budget...." He then gives you a thick, fat checkbook with blank checks — but all pre-signed. "Just put whatever figure you need." Yes, my friend, He has given you all that you need for success. *Start using God's checkbook now!*

Write your dreams.

Be the Scriptwriter of your life.

Truly Rich Principle:
You have the power to create the life you want.

CHAPTER 24

Write Down Your Dreams

There are no limits to the mind except those that we acknowledge.
— Napoleon Hill

I remember that day as though it were yesterday.

One night in 1997, I came home from a prayer meeting all revved up. I had a powerful thought in my mind: God has given us the power to decide what kind of life we want.

At 11 p.m., I couldn't sleep. If God really gave me the power to define my life, then I wanted to do it. I've already wasted so many years letting things happen to me.

So on that fateful night, I sat down in front of my computer, and with my heart pounding in my chest, I wrote down my dreams. I couldn't stop. My fingers dribbled on my keyboard furiously, I was waiting for it to smoke.

I didn't stop until it was 3 a.m. and finished writing 15 pages of my dreams for the future.

I wrote down everything I wanted to do with my life.

I wrote down how much money I'd earn each year for the next 30 years. I wrote down outrageous amounts. I wrote down every possible income stream that I'd use to earn that money. And I also wrote down how much money I'd give away.

For my family life, I wrote, "I'll be the greatest husband my wife can ever have" and "I'll be the greatest father my children can ever have."

It was so detailed, I wrote down stuff like, "I'll kiss my wife seven times a day" and "I'll bring her out on a romantic date at least once a week," and "I'll play with my children every day." I described myself at 82 years old — during my golden wedding anniversary — surrounded by my children and grandchildren. The vision took my breath away.

I wrote down goals for my physical health and intellectual growth, like, "I will exercise daily" and "I will read three books a week...."

I also wrote down my ministry goals. That I will author bestselling books, that I will broadcast God's love through a TV show and a radio program, even if I had no idea how I could pay for the astronomical production costs.

Writing my dreams was fantastic. It made me see in vivid color what I wanted to do with my life. It opened my mind to what was possible.

What has happened these past 10 years?

So far, I have written eight bestselling books.

I now have a weekly TV show, a daily radio program and a daily reality show on the Internet that is seen all over the world.

Each year, I have reached my outrageous financial goals.

And I wish to report to you that I do kiss my wife seven times a day. (Yes, even when I don't feel like kissing her.) I do bring her out on a romantic date once a week.

I remember one date. In the middle of our dessert, she reached for my hand, clasped it, looked me in the eye and said, "Bo, you are a great husband."

My heart fluttered inside me like it had wings. And I wanted to tell her, "That's in page 3, paragraph 4." Yes, I knew my Life Dreams document by heart.

Why do I believe in the power of writing down our dreams?

I stumbled upon this study made in Harvard. In 1957, they asked Harvard graduates whether they write their dreams. Only three percent of the entire batch answered yes. Twenty years later, in 1977, they went back to these same graduates, and what they learned astounded them. The most successful among the entire batch were the same three percent who wrote down their goals 20 years ago!

Writing our dreams has a powerful effect on our brain.

It causes our minds to open up to opportunities that will help us reach our goals — opportunities that we wouldn't have seen if we didn't create a graphic vision of our future.

Write down your dreams.

CHAPTER 25

Read Your Dreams Every Day

People are not lazy. They simply have impotent goals—
that is, goals that do not inspire them.
— Anthony Robbins

Let me now give you one of the most powerful success habits of my life.

Since 1997, I've *read* my Life Dreams every day.

That 15-page document I talked about in the previous chapter? That's what I read every single day before I do anything else.

Each morning, as part of my prayer, I read my dreams and present them to God one more time. I declare it anew to myself, to the world, to the universe. I remind myself of my future.

It's so powerful, I wake up each morning knowing exactly what I want to do with my life.

Each morning, I'm like a bullet shooting through a barrel of a gun. I know my target. I know my aim. I know where I'm going. I know what I'm supposed to do.

This is especially crucial when obstacles come along my path. These blocks could be so gigantic and menacing, I lose sight of my goal. But reading my dreams every day gives me back my vision.

So writing your dreams is fantastic. By itself, it already unlocks the blessings of the universe to your life. By writing down your dreams, you open yourself to life's river of abundance.

But when you read what you wrote down every day, you multiply the power of that river tenfold.

I've got my Life Dreams document in my computer.

So all I do is click on its icon each day and it appears on the screen.

Others have made use of my *Life Dreams Success Journal,* putting it beside their Bible or *Companion.*[1] Each day, after reading God's Word, they declare their Life Dreams anew to the universe.

Read your dreams every day.

Truly Rich Principle:
By writing down your dreams, you open yourself to life's river of abundance. But when you read what you wrote down daily, you multiply the power of that river tenfold.

[1] *Companion* is a daily Scripture diary that I developed to help people read the Bible every day. It's based on the Mass readings and has helpful comments, so you can understand God's Word better. For more information, go to **www.shepherdsvoice.com.ph** or call (632) 725-9999.

CHAPTER 26

Apply the Power of Focus

Every great man has become great, every successful man has succeeded, in proportion as he has confined his powers to one particular channel.
— Orison Swett Marden

In other words, what I'm asking you to do is apply the Law of Focus.

The Law of Focus is like the Law of Gravity. It never fails. It has no exceptions.

The Law of Focus states that *what you focus on grows.*

Let me give you a simple example.

One day, when my wife was pregnant and had a tummy the size of a huge watermelon, we were walking through the mall. After a few minutes of strolling, she turned to me and said, "Bo, haven't you noticed? There are so many pregnant women in the mall today. I've counted more than 10 already!"

Were there really more pregnant women at that particular time? No. She just noticed them more because that was her focus. When your tummy is the size of a watermelon, how can it not be your focus?

So if each day, you focus on the bad things happening in your life, I can assure you that these bad things will keep on growing. Because you focus on them, you'll be an expert at spotting them a mile away — and you'll be more miserable than ever. If all you do is complain and bicker and criticize, without a shadow of a doubt, you'll grow into an old goat that no one wants to be with and your death will be a happy event in the family.

But if each day, you focus on the good things happening to your life — and begin and end each day counting your blessings, then this is what will happen: Your blessings will increase! You'll be an expert at seeing more of them. And your positive attitude will actually attract new blessings into your life.

That's why the Bible insists that we be grateful and "be thankful in all circumstances."[1]

[1] 1 Thessalonians 5:18

But wait a minute. How does this apply to money?

Do you know why many spiritual people don't get rich? Because they don't focus on money. And what you don't focus on has very little chance of growing. Because spiritual persons focus on their spiritual life, and *only* on their spiritual life. And they become poor in the other areas.

There's nothing wrong with that. Unless of course you're a father raising your kids, and there's no money to put food on the table, or buy medicines when they get sick.

This is the message of this book: Even if you're a spiritual person, give yourself permission to focus on money. Start thinking about money, reading about money, talking about money, learning about money — but always see money from the lens of your spiritual life.

Yes, put God first and all your money as His servant.

But you still need to give some of your time to focus on money, or it won't grow.

Here's the most powerful way I know of focusing on money: Have a financial goal for each year, write it down in your Life Dreams, and read it every day.

And even while you sleep, your brain will search far and wide, looking for ways to fulfill those financial goals. You'll be surprised at how opportunities will open up before you. Actually, many of them were already there. But because you weren't focused, you didn't notice them, waiting to be discovered.

When Jim Carrey was a struggling, broke, stand-up comedian in small comedy clubs, he wrote a $10 million check with the words, "For services rendered" underneath. He read this check every day. Years later, Jim Carrey would be earning $20 million per movie.

Apply the Power of Focus.

Truly Rich Principle:
You'll be surprised at how money-making opportunities will open up before you. Actually, they're already there, waiting for you to discover them.

CHAPTER 27

Apply the Power of Attraction

Imagination is everything.
— Albert Einstein

On her 75th birthday, I visited *Tita* Julie Gandiongco of Julie's Bakeshop.

She's such a simple, very down-to-earth, beautiful woman — you'd never think she owned a bread empire.

Let me tell you her inspiring story.

Tita Julie was a 46-year-old housewife who had zero business experience and had no college degree when she started a little canteen in a factory. It was her first business. Before this, she just stayed home and took care of the kids.

But at the late age of 50 (when others her age look forward to retirement and taking it easy), she started her first bakeshop. And then another. And then another still.

Today, Julie's Bakeshop has 500 plus bakeshops all over the country.

Recently, her bakeshop won the Best Franchisee Award.

When I talked to her, she told me of a core belief that blew me away. She said, "Whatever I need comes to me."

Wow. What a powerful belief.

Imagine if each morning, we say those words: "Whatever I need comes to me."

This is the Law of Attraction at work — also called the Law of Focus.

And let me repeat, it's an unbreakable principle of this universe. No exceptions.

The Law of Attraction states that you attract to your life your predominant thoughts.

Let me give you the secret of this universe: **Your thoughts create things.**

Your thoughts aren't powerless fluff that come in and go out of your brain.

Your thoughts actually produce your reality.

So if every day, all you do is think about your poverty and complain about how poor you are, you're creating more poverty in your life — guaranteed! You'll become poorer and poorer.

Remember: The universe adjusts to your expectations.

If you see yourself as a poor person trapped in your poverty, the universe will oblige and give you what you are even half-expecting — that you will remain in your poverty forever.

Do you want to escape your poverty?

Then start changing your daily, predominant thoughts.

Start thinking of yourself as a rich person, enjoying wealth, abundance and prosperity. Imagine! Picture yourself! Feel it!

See yourself earning a specific amount of money each month.

See yourself giving generously to God a specific amount each month.

Feel the incredible freedom of having more than enough to share.

And be totally committed to making that dream a reality.

Here's a favorite fantasy I have: I no longer search for money. Money searches for me. How? Through the Law of Attraction, I've become a money magnet.

And I'm seeing this happen in my life.

Opportunities to earn money appear in front of me with such speed, I'm overwhelmed by them.

Apply the Power of Attraction.

Truly Rich Principle:
The universe adjusts to your expectations. So instead of you searching for money, let money search for you. Attract money. Become a money magnet.

5 SECRET

Raise Your Financial I.Q.

Blessed is the man who finds wisdom, the man who gains understanding, for she is more profitable than silver and yields better returns than gold. She is more precious than rubies; nothing you desire can compare with her.
— Proverbs 3:13-15

At the start of this book, I mentioned that there are three big problems why people don't get rich:

1. People *subconsciously* don't like to get rich.
2. People are financially stupid.
3. People don't ride *something* to wealth.

I believe that the first problem is the biggest problem of all.

That's why I spent the first 4 Secrets to solve that problem.

To solve the first problem — that people *subconsciously* don't like to get rich — you need to apply all four Secrets:

Secret #1: *Be Responsible for Your Financial Success.*
Secret #2: *Enlarge Your Psychological Wallet.*
Secret #3: *Get Rid of Crazy Religious Beliefs.*

Secret #4: *Be Totally Committed to Your Dreams.*

In Secret #5, *Raise Your Financial I.Q.,* I will now address the second problem on why people don't get rich — because they don't know how.

This section will blow your mind — on how simple it is to make money. You don't have to be a brilliant PhD holder to get it. You just need to learn very simple concepts that will change your financial life forever.

In the next few pages, you will learn how money works.

Raise your financial I.Q.

CHAPTER 28

Financial Ignorance Is Expensive

The number one problem in today's generation and economy is the lack of financial literacy.
— Alan Greenspan

Some people think buying a book like this is expensive.

I also give financial seminars and people think the price we charge is too high.

If you think financial wisdom is expensive, then try ignorance.

You'll realize it's a million times more expensive.

For example, in the past 10 years, I've lost a lot of money. Simply because I was stupid about money.

After getting married, I was able to scrape a decent amount of savings into our bank account every month. And with some very generous gifts from our *ninangs*[1] during our wedding, after a few years, my savings reached P200,000 plus. (Sssshh. Don't laugh too hard.)

That was when a friend asked me if I would like to put my money in the investment company she was working for. "You'll earn two percent a month," she said, "and you'll help me earn a commission from your investment!"

And instantly, I invested our P200,000. After all, two percent a month came down to 24 percent a year — so much higher than the banks' interest.

That was also the time when my wife finally got pregnant.

The thought of becoming a father was an incredible feeling.

But together with my excitement was the stark realization that the baby would now be totally dependent on my finances for the next 20 years of his life.

Sheesh. That thought sent chills down my spine.

We borrowed a wooden crib from a cousin and prepared P20,000

[1] godmothers

for the birth of our baby. We were ready, or so I thought.

During the delivery, my wife suffered heart palpitations reaching 200 beats per minute and the doctor ordered an emergency Caesarian operation.

Yes, I almost lost my wife and baby. That emergency operation saved their lives.

After three days of confinement, I received the bill from the hospital: P56,000.

Gulp.

Have you ever received a solid punch straight to your solar plexus?

That was how I felt at that moment.

So I called my friend and asked if I could get my investment back. Perhaps just P40,000 of my P200,000 to pay the hospital bill.

She said, "I'll try...."

"Try? Why try? Isn't that my money?" I asked, "I need to pay the hospital."

"It isn't that simple," she explained. "Your money is being used."

"What do they use it for? Who owns this company anyway? How long have they been in business?" (Do you see how wise I was? I was asking these questions *after* I invested my money.)

"We're a small firm that lends money to tricycle drivers."

"Wha...." Have you ever seen a cat staring at the headlights of an oncoming truck? That's how I looked.

"And collection hasn't been very good," my friend's mutter was barely audible.

"So that means..."

"Uh, that means we'll have to wait for new investors to come in before we can return a part of your money."

In other words, I waited three years for nothing. After that the company closed, folded up, crashed, disintegrated, imploded, sunk to the depths of the earth, vanished into thin air.

With my P200,000 with them.

Don't you see?

I was financially dumb.

Let me give you my credentials: My I.Q. is 132, I have above-average social skills, I finished Philosophy in college, I took post-graduate courses in Theology, I founded four organizations, and I'm a more-or-less overall wholesome guy.... But all these don't take away the fact that

I was a *financial nincompoop.*

I was 100 percent financially illiterate!

Here's what I found out:

You could be a doctor with three PhDs behind your name.

You could be an engineer building huge bridges in your spare time.

You could be a very holy person, praying three hours a day.

You could be a scientist inventing the first car that runs on spit.

You could be 97 years old.

You could be an extremely loving saint.

You could be a diva with the voice of Celine Dion.

But you could also be financially illiterate.

A world-renowned surgeon doesn't open up a busted TV set and say, "I operate on people, I guess operating on machines would be a breeze." No, it won't be. It's a totally different world.

So it is with money.

Knowing how money works is a totally different field of expertise.

Financial ignorance is expensive.

> Truly Rich Principle:
> **Knowing how money works is a totally different field of expertise.**

CHAPTER 29

Look for Financial Mentors

Study anyone who's great, and you'll find that they apprenticed to a master or several masters. Therefore, if you want to achieve greatness... you must apprentice to a master.

— Robert Allen

Holding your baby in your hands is one of the sweetest delights known to mankind. Unless, of course, he starts peeing all over you.

One day, as I hugged my baby and placed his face on my cheek (and as I directed his boy-part to point somewhere else just in case), I began to think of his education. He'll be so bright, I imagined him taking up Molecular Biology, Journalism, Fine Arts and Law, all at the same time.

So like good parents that we were, we bought him an educational plan for his grade school and high school education from a pre-need company.

With our eyes closed (wondering how in the world we would afford it), we signed up for a P9,000 a month payment plan for the next five years. It was steep, but we wanted to give him the best. So we did it.

During that time, I was already getting into small businesses.

I failed in many of them (I'll tell you more about that later), but one started earning. Each month, I kept its earnings. After two years, I collected P200,000. Yipee!

Again, not knowing enough about money, I invested the P200,000 *at the same pre-need company* where I bought my educational plan, this time as a pension fund.

Fast forward to a few years later. As we neared the end of our educational plan's payments, we read a very disturbing article in the newspaper: Nine pre-need companies in the Philippines could no longer pay the tuition fees of their plan holders.

Yikes.

Surely, ours wasn't included, right?

Wrong. Ours was on the list.

To this day, that company is still fighting for its life.

I invested P740,000 in that company and I may never see it again.

Once upon a time, there were 92 pre-need companies in the Philippines.

By the year 2005, there were 32 left.[1]

These companies are only partly to blame for my financial loss.

I lost my money because I lacked financial education. I didn't research enough, and didn't have financial mentors to guide me. For years, financial experts were already sounding the alarm, warning people of the coming collapse. But I didn't listen because I didn't know who to listen to.

Today, I now have financial mentors that surround me. I don't make big investment decisions without their counsel.

To find them, I had to pray for them, search for them, and invest time and energy to pursue the best. But once I found them, they powerfully blessed my financial life.

How do you find these mentors?

Look around for financially successful people.

I don't care if your uncle has a PhD in Economics. If his own personal finances are in shambles, he's not your financial mentor. I don't care if your aunt gives you a business card that says she's a financial advisor, if she has a lot of bad debts and doesn't invest her own money, she's not your financial mentor.

Swallow this hard pill: The proof of real financial wisdom is in the money.

Look for financial mentors.

Truly Rich Principle:
Who should be your financial mentor?
Follow the money.

[1] But I believe this is better because the strongest have remained. The pre-need companies who are still standing to this day have passed the strict standards that the government has set to safeguard the investing public.

CHAPTER 30

Avoid Bad Debt Like Bad Bacteria

Too many people spend money they haven't earned, to buy things they don't want, to impress people they don't like.
— Will Rogers

Not all debt is bad.

There is such a thing as good debt and bad debt — just as there are good bacteria and bad bacteria.

In the bestselling book *Rich Dad, Poor Dad,* Robert Kiyosaki explains that good debt is when we buy things that put money into our pocket. And bad debt is when we buy things that take money away from our pockets.

If I get a loan to buy a rental apartment, and the tenant pays me each month for the use of that apartment, that's good debt.

If I get a loan to buy a wide-screen TV for my personal enjoyment, that's what you call bad debt. Because it doesn't put money into my pocket.

Friend, let me ask you: What kind of debts do you have?

If you have bad debt, make a goal now to get out of it and give yourself a specific deadline.

Face the mirror and shout out loud: "I'm going to be financially free!" Make it your goal, make it your prayer, make it your battle cry.

Do you know what the greatest magic in the world is? Albert Einstein said that the greatest magic in the world is *daily compounded interest.*

Isn't that weird? You'd expect Einstein to say something like "nuclear energy" or "the theory of relativity," but that's not what he said.

Why is daily compounded interest the greatest magic?

Because the results are explosive and simply out of this world.

Here's the bad news: If you have bad debt, you make the "greatest magic in the world" your powerful enemy. You don't want that to happen. Because this enemy will eat you alive.

So a critical step to becoming rich is to get out of bad debt as fast as possible. *Get this enemy called daily compounded interest to join your side.* (More on this later.)

If you're buried under a lot of debt, here are five crucial actions you need to make:

1. Declare Your Freedom Day

If you think about all your debts, it'll kill your spirit. (Remember what I said? What you focus on grows.) So focus instead on your coming freedom. Write a deadline when you'll be financially free. Call it your Freedom Day and plan for a big celebration. Read this goal daily, think about it daily, pray for it daily. Sleep with it, walk with it, work with it, eat with it.

2. Create New Ways of Pleasure

Discover new habits of simple joys. Examine your lifestyle. Have you been spending more than you're actually earning? It's time to cut back on things you can do without. That extra dress. That dinner out. That movie. And get the same amount of joy (or even more) from free — or almost free — pleasures. A picnic in the park. A quiet read in the library. A walk around the neighborhood.

3. Schedule Your Steps to Freedom

With your increased savings from a simpler lifestyle, sit down and write how much you can set aside each month to pay your debts. Schedule all payments, starting with high-interest loans first. And if you can, transfer high-interest loans to low-interest loans.

4. Don't Borrow When You Can't Afford It—Period!

Don't borrow to buy consumer goods ever again. If you don't have money right now to buy it, then don't buy it. If the credit card in your wallet is a huge temptation, then get rid of it until you acquire discipline.

5. Negotiate with Your Creditors

See your creditors regularly — assure them you'll pay — but negotiate to reduce their interest rates. I've learned that because human beings run banks and other lending institutions, and because these same flesh-and-blood people make the policies, everything is negotiable. Everything. Don't back down simply because they say, "It's the policy here that we don't decrease interest rates." Persevere.

Avoid bad debt like bad bacteria.

CHAPTER 31

Protect Yourself

I detest insurance agents; They keep telling me I will die someday, which is not so.
— Stephen Leacock, comedian

In life, you have two major problems when it comes to money.

According to Xuan Nguyen, you can either: (1) die too young or, (2) live too long. Here's the key: Both problems need to be addressed.

If you die too young, you'll be leaving behind people that are dependent on your income. What will happen to them? You need to provide for them even after your death.

If you live too long, and live 30 years after your retirement, will you have enough savings to maintain your needs for the next 30 years? You'll need to provide for your old age.

Solving one problem won't be enough. You need to solve both. And you can. So if I "die too young" when my savings are still low and my responsibilities are still high, I can only solve that by having some type of "protection." If I get physically handicapped or I suddenly die, my wife and kids would need "income replacement." That can only come from buying insurance.

Now I know some people are allergic to that word. If you're sitting on a bus and the person beside you suddenly introduces himself as an insurance agent, do you quickly go down the bus and walk instead?

Here's another problem. I know some Christians who actually condemn insurance as a lack of trust in God.

That's pure organic fertilizer. (That's my more respectful way of saying "horse manure.")

If insurance means not trusting God, then we also shouldn't put fire escapes in our windows and fire extinguishers in our homes because God will protect us from all fires. Then we shouldn't also have locks in our doors and alarms in our cars because God will protect us from all thieves. Then we shouldn't take vitamins because God will keep us healthy.

Absolutely absurd.

I believe that God protects our families through this blessing called insurance.

Get protection.

Truly Rich Principle:
I believe that God protects our families through this blessing called insurance.

CHAPTER 32

Protect Yourself Adequately

A rich man's wealth is his strong city, like a high wall protecting him.
— Proverbs 18:11

If you're thinking, "I've bought enough insurance, I'll skip this chapter," please don't. Because many Filipinos are grossly underinsured.

I've heard horror stories of popular politicians, great doctors and top-earning executives, who died in decrepit government hospitals. They left absolutely nothing to their families because their personal funds were wiped out by their lingering illness — and they had no more insurance. You'd think these intelligent men and women were wise enough to buy insurance. But no. The politician had great political wisdom, the doctor had great medical wisdom, the executive had great corporate wisdom — but that's not equal to having great financial wisdom. Which is what this book is all about.

So how much insurance do you really need?

Here's the formula: Multiply your annual expenses by 10. So if you spend P100,000 a year, you need P1 million insurance. If you spend P500,000 a year, then you need P5 million insurance. If you spend P1 million a year, then you need P10 million. (So, are you underinsured?)

Why that amount?

This is how it works: Let's say each year, you spend P500,000 for your family's needs. So you get a P5 million insurance. In the event of your death, the insurance company gives P5 million to the family you left behind.

Now, your family could spend that amount little by little until it becomes smoke.

Or, your family could become financially wise by investing the entire amount in a fund (more on this later) that earns 10 percent a year. That'll give them P500,000 a year which, if you notice, *is the same amount your family was spending while you were alive.* So they're provided for the rest of their lives. Isn't that lovely?

Now there are a plethora of insurance products out there.

So the big question is: What kind of insurance do you need?

It depends on your specific needs and what age you're in. There are now many insurance products for the varied situations you're in, so explore. A word of advice: Whole life insurance can be a rip-off if you put all your money into it. (Yes, you need a little of whole life so that you're insured after the age of 65.) For most of us, the best insurance is term insurance. It's much cheaper than whole life, and you can invest the rest into investment vehicles I'll discuss later in this book.

Look also for good health insurance for yourself. You don't want to scramble for money when you need to be hospitalized.

And get other insurance products for other areas of your life.

Here's your goal: You want to be self-insured. You want your money to grow year after year to a point where you no longer need insurance.

How do you do that?

By increasing your own retirement fund which we will discuss in the next chapter.

Protect yourself adequately.

CHAPTER 33

Build Your Retirement Fund Now

I have enough money to last me the rest of my life—
unless I buy something.
— Jackie Mason

Five million pesos. That's a lot of moolah.

That was how much Manny was getting for his retirement — and he salivated every time he thought about it. He worked in the same company for 34 years and was looking forward to planting vegetables in his little garden and having quiet dates with his wife while sipping brewed coffee and doughnuts together — using their senior citizen cards for their 20 percent discount.

Of course, his P1 million debt to the company will get paid first. Many years ago, he borrowed money to build his house and buy his car.

Manny's heart raced with delight when he saw the P4 million deposited in his bank account. Wow, he could now do all the things he wanted to do.

First things first. He'll restore his 17-year-old house. For the longest time, Manny wanted to fix the leaking roof, retile the bathrooms and replace the kitchen cabinets. He also added a veranda at the back (with a wooden swing set) and an extra recreation room. Cost: P1 million.

Next, buy his dream car. Cost: P1 million.

After one year, Manny had P2 million left in his bank account.

At first, he was spending P50,000 a month. Later on, as he saw his money shrinking, he began to panic. He downgraded his lifestyle and spent P30,000 a month, and later still, P20,000 a month.

Five years later, at the age of 65, he had nothing in the bank.

He was forced to sell his house and move to a rented apartment.

That money lasted for another five years.

When he reached 70, Manny had to totally depend on his children. He hated the idea. But he had no choice. His children, though saddled with their own problems, had to fork out P15,000 a month for their parents.

Manny would live like this for the next 14 years, until he died at age 84.

In the previous chapter, I said that there were two problems in life: (1) dying too young, and (2) living too long. Manny had the problem of living too long.

For the first problem of dying too young, the solution is having protection or insurance. For the second problem of living too long, the solution is to build your own retirement fund now.

Friend, Manny is not one person. He's a composite character I created from the many retired people I've met through the years. Believe me, it's a very painful sight to see, watching someone go down to poverty and dependence.

Simply because they didn't prepare for their retirement.

According to many surveys on people above the age of 65 (rounded off figures)...

1. **Around 40 percent have to keep on working to survive.**
   I don't mind working till I'm 90 years old — because I love working. But to have to keep on working at 70, or 80, or 90 so that I have something to eat? What if my health can't keep up with my job? What will happen to me? But that's the life of millions of old people.

2. **Around 30 percent depend on their relatives to survive.**
   I think every parent I've talked to doesn't want to be a burden to their children. And we want the freedom to have our own money—so that we can do what we want to do in our old age. Can you imagine having to call up your kids each month to ask for money? But that's what millions of aging parents have to do to live each day.

3. **Around 20 percent depend only on their SSS or GSIS pension fund to survive.**
   My father worked for his company for 40 years. He retired as assistant vice president, so his SSS contributions were the maximum you could contribute. But to this day, he receives

P4,000 a month. It isn't even enough for an herbal drink I buy for him each month. Thankfully, my father saved enough and doesn't depend on his pension to survive.

4. **Eight percent depend on charitable institutions to survive.**
   That's why I built Anawim, our home for the abandoned elderly. You'd be surprised at the kind of people who end up in our care. We have retired laundry women, retired domestic helpers and retired farmers who grew old and penniless. That's not surprising. But we also have retired teachers, retired school principals, retired book authors, retired mechanics, a retired TV director, even a retired dentist. After earning probably millions throughout their life, they found themselves without a home and starving to death.

5. **Two percent are financially independent.**
   Friend, I want you to be totally committed to be part of this two percent when you reach 65. And I know of only one way to be part of this small group: Build your retirement fund now. I don't care if you're 30 years old, 25 years old, or even 18 years old. You've got to start building your retirement fund now. Not tomorrow, not next week, not next year, but now.

In the next few chapters, I'll teach you how.

Build your retirement fund now.

Truly Rich Principle:
You've got to start building your retirement fund now. Not tomorrow, not next week, not next year, but now.

CHAPTER 34

Automatically Save 20 Percent of Your Monthly Income

A part of all you earn is yours to keep, and if you cannot save money, the seeds of greatness are not in you.
— W. Clement Stone

Do you know the common habit of a permanently poor person?

After receiving his salary, he pays his bills right away.

Wrong move.

Here's what rich people (and potentially rich people) do: After receiving their salary, *they save first* — and then pay their bills second.

I recommend that you give your first 10 percent to God (more on this later), give your next 20 percent for yourself as your retirement fund, and live on 70 percent of your income.

I know what you're thinking: "Bo, are you nuts? How can I live on 70 percent? I now live on 110 percent of my income!"

Here's my answer: If there's a will, there's a way. If you really want something bad enough, nothing is impossible. Do you want to be part of that two percent of people above 65 who are financially independent? Then do it. (If you want more ideas on how to do this, you can read my two previous books, *Simplify and Live the Good Life,* and *Simplify and Create Abundance.* Go to your nearest bookstore or log on to **www.bosanchez.ph** and click on books and magazines.)

Besides, in the later chapters, I'll teach you how to *increase* your income, so living on 70 percent of your income will be easy.

But right now, I want you to sit down and write down how much 20 percent of your income is. Make it *automatic.* Write down postdated checks to yourself if you have to. Month after month, make it happen. Every time you receive your salary, get 20 percent and put it into your retirement fund.

My idea of saving 20 percent of your monthly income comes from the Bible. When Joseph was overseer of Egypt, he prepared for famine by saving a "fifth of the produce." So when famine came, Egypt was the only country that had food — and the peoples of other nations came to them to buy grain.

> *Let Pharaoh proceed to appoint overseers over the land, and take the fifth part of the produce of the land of Egypt during the seven plenteous years. And let them gather all the food of these good years that are coming, and lay up grain under the authority of Pharaoh for food in the cities, and let them keep it. That food shall be a reserve for the land against the seven years of famine which are to befall the land of Egypt, so that the land may not perish through the famine.*
>
> — Genesis 41:34-36

Famine will always happen.

How do you protect yourself from famine — which would be the future decades of your life when you're no longer earning?

By saving 20 percent of your income *now* while you are earning.

In the next chapter, I'll explain why doing this early will create a huge retirement fund that will bless your life.

Automatically save 20 percent of your monthly income.

> Truly Rich Principle:
> **Famine will always come. So prepare for it.**

CHAPTER 35

Invest as Early as You Can

Let me tell you a fascinating story.

One day, a 22-year-old good-looking guy named Pepe read about this principle of saving 20 percent of his income. He was earning the small salary of P8,000 a month, but he decided to save P1,600 a month anyway. That came to about P20,000 a year. Being a financially wise man, he invested it in a place that gave him 12 percent interest per year. Pepe saved P20,000 every year until he reached the age of 27.

That was when he met the pretty Pilar — a woman who was exactly his age. (They even had the same birthday.) Pepe discovered that she didn't save, so he encouraged her to do what he was doing.

So Pilar also started saving P20,000 a year at age 28, putting her money at the same place where Pepe invested his — earning 12 percent interest a year.

But at that same year, Pepe left for China to be a lay missionary and couldn't save anymore.

After six years, Pilar had saved exactly the same amount of money as Pepe did. But at the age of 33, Pepe called her up and said, "We need someone like you in China. Please come and be a lay missionary like me!" So she went, and could no longer save as well.

At the age of 62, both Pepe and Pilar came back to the Philippines for good.

Upon deplaning, Pepe did the unexpected. He planted one knee on the tarmac and said, "Pilar, will you marry me?"

Pilar wiped a tear and said, "Gosh, I've waited for this proposal for 40 years. Yes, Pepe, even if we have no money, I will marry you!" And they hugged each other.

Pepe however said, "Well, I think we have a little money. Remember when we were in our 20s and 30s? We saved some money."

Pilar said, "That was really small. I remember saving P20,000 for six years. That's only P120,000."

Pepe smiled, "Hey, me, too! I also saved P120,000. I think that's enough for the wedding!"

So excitedly, Pepe and Pilar marched to the office where they invested their money years ago.

"Excuse me, sir," Pilar said, "I'm Pilar and I'd like to know how much money I have."

The guy in front of the computer said, "Let me see...." After a lot of suspense he said, "Aha, here it is. My records show that you have P4.8 million."

Pilar fainted.

When she recovered, she told Pepe, "You'll probably have the same amount of money! Ask them."

Pepe asked, "Sir, my name is Pepe, and I'd like to know how much money I have."

The guy looks at his computer files and says, "According to my records, you have P9.6 million."

Pilar fainted again.

She said, "That's impossible. We put the same amount of money! Each of us put P120,000. Why is his money double that of mine?"

The answer came, "Because Pepe saved six years before you did."

And so Pepe and Pilar had a grand wedding and lived happily ever after.

Remember what Albert Einstein said about the greatest magic in the world? Daily compounded interest worked day and night for Pepe and Pilar.

Here's the table of computations for Pepe's and Pilar's investments:[1]

Pepe:				Pilar:		
Age	**Savings**	**Total**		**Age**	**Savings**	**Total**
22	20,000	22,400		22	0	0
23	20,000	47,490		23	0	0
24	20,000	75,590		24	0	0
25	20,000	107,060		25	0	0
26	20,000	142,300		26	0	0
27	20,000	181,780		27	0	0
28	0	203,590		28	20,000	22,400

[1] I wish to thank the *International Marketing Group* for this table (used with permission). I just added the story to put the flesh-and-blood on these numbers.

29	0	228,030	29	20,000	47,490
30	0	255,390	30	20,000	75,590
31	0	286,030	31	20,000	107,060
32	0	320,360	32	20,000	142,300
33	0	358,800	33	20,000	181,780
28	0	401,860	28	0	203,590
29	0	450,080	29	0	228,030
30	0	504,090	30	0	255,390
31	0	564,580	31	0	286,030
32	0	632,330	32	0	320,360
33	0	708,210	33	0	358,800
34	0	793,200	34	0	401,860
35	0	888,380	35	0	450,080
36	0	994,990	36	0	504,090
37	0	1,114,390	37	0	532,330
62	0	P9.6M	62	0	P4.8M

What's the lesson of this story?

Here it is: Don't get married at 62.

I'm kidding.

There are actually two very important lessons in this story:

Lesson #1: The earlier you save, the better.

Lesson #2: You need to know where to invest your savings.

Banks are good places to put our emergency funds and business funds. But never put your retirement and long-term savings there. It won't work. (I'll explain later why.)

Save first and spend later.

CHAPTER 36

Don't Put Your Retirement Fund in the Bank

A peso goes a long way now.
You can carry it around for days without finding a thing it will buy.
— Anonymous

When I was a kid, a bus ride cost 25 centavos.

Today, the same bus ride costs seven pesos.

What happened? In one word, inflation.

Over time, your money loses its purchasing power.

How much? It loses around seven percent a year.

Do you now see how futile it is to put your savings in the bank? As of this writing, a savings account in a major bank promises you one percent interest, while a time deposit promises five percent interest. These aren't enough to fight inflation. At the end of the year, your money would still have decreased in purchasing power.

What should you do?

Here's the key: *Differentiate your emergency fund from your retirement fund.* Put your emergency fund — around three to six months of your salary — in the bank. That's for quick withdrawals.

But not your retirement fund.

When it comes to money, there are really only three kinds of people in this world: (1) Spender, (2) Saver, and (3) Investor. And sadly, only one of these three will win in the money game. Which one are you?

Let me introduce them to you by way of a story.

James, Jim and John were salesmen. The three of them landed a huge deal. And their company gave each of them a P100,000 commission check. They were totally blown away by their luck, but they used their money in very different ways. Because James was a Spender, Jim was a Saver, and John was an Investor.

1. Spender

James was the Spender.

Upon receiving his check, James encashed it, and went straight to a fancy restaurant and invited all his friends to celebrate his good fortune. Later that day, he bought himself a new hi-tech cell phone, nifty clothes and a brand new pair of designer shoes. The next day, he took a holiday trip to Boracay.

In three days, James had nothing left from the P100,000 commission.

This is the story of his life. After many years of working, he has no savings to show, but he has many credit card debts.

We see Spenders everywhere, and I hope you're not one of them.

2. Saver

Jim was the Saver.

Jim walked straight to the bank with his P100,000 check.

He approached the friendly bank teller with a smile and said, "Miss, I don't plan to touch my money for a long time. It's P100,000. How much interest will you give me?"

She nodded and said, "Let's put it at a time deposit account. We'll give you five percent interest a year. That's the highest we can give you, sir."

"Okay!" he agreed, signed the deposit slip, and walked out happy.

Thirty-six years later, he was 65 years old. He retired at age 60, got his retirement package, spent it in five years, and was now totally broke. That was when he remembered his time deposit. He visited his bank.

He saw the same friendly teller "Hi, I deposited P100,000 some 36 years ago," he said, "and I'm finally withdrawing it. How much is it now?"

"Just a minute, sir," she looked at her computer, and after a few minutes looked up and said, "Sir, you now have P400,000."

The retired salesman blinked hard. "After 36 years, it's only grown to P400,000? Perhaps you've made a mistake, miss."

"I'm no longer a miss, sir. *Lola na ako.*[1] And no, there's no mistake...."

I pity Savers. Savers are good, disciplined, honest people.

But Savers still don't win in the money game.

3. Investor

John was the Investor.

He doesn't go straight to the bank. He goes to *where the bank puts their money.* In other words, he bypasses the bank.

Out of the three salesmen, only John has raised his financial I.Q. He learned that the bank puts a part of their money in investment vehicles like mutual funds, bond funds, equity funds and stocks. So he thought, if it's good for them, why not for me?

So John takes a few days researching for the best mutual fund investments in the country and visits one of them.

He approaches the lady behind the desk and says, "I've never done this before but I want to invest in mutual funds. How much interest will you give me?"

The lady shook her head. "Unlike banks, we don't guarantee our interest rates. They depend on the ups and downs of the market."

"Isn't that scary?" John raised his eyebrow.

"It is — if you plan to invest for only a short period of time. But if you plan to invest long term and 'forget' about it, it won't be scary. Like for the past years, we've given our investors an average of nine percent to 12 percent growth."

"Yes, I do plan to invest for the long term," he says, "but do I have to invest millions to join your mutual fund? I don't have millions."

She laughed. "Sir, the minimum is P5,000 per investment."

His eyes bulged. "What? That small? Then anyone can invest!"

"Mutual funds are the great equalizer. Some call it the secret of the rich which is now available to the poor. Banks don't treat people equally, but we do. Someone who puts P5 million in the bank gets a higher interest than someone who puts P5,000. But in mutual funds, it doesn't matter how much you put in. Five

[1] I'm a grandma now.

million or P5,000, you earn the same interest."

"This is incredible," he says. "Why don't people know about this?"

She said, "In the Philippines, less than one percent of Filipinos invest in mutual funds, while 99 percent invest in banks. But in America today, 70 percent already invest in mutual funds, while 30 percent invest in banks only. The Philippines is 30 years behind America, but we're getting there…."

So John invested his P100,000 and left happy.

Thirty-six years later, at the age of 65, John wanted his investment back. So he walked into the same mutual fund company and saw the same lady behind her desk. He asked her, "How did my investment fare the past 36 years?"

The lady said, "To be honest, there were bad years and good years. There were years your money earned only seven percent but there were great years when your money earned 20 percent and more. In the past 36 years, you averaged 12 percent a year."

"Is that good?" he asked.

"According to my records," she smiled, "your original P100,000 has now grown to P6.4 million. Now *you* tell me if that is good," she winked.

"That's very good!" John grinned from ear to ear.

Friend, now you know why banks have nice, tall, expensive buildings.

They get your P100,000 and invest it in an investment vehicle where they earn P6.4 million, and then return to you the P400,000.

How much did they earn? Six million.

So next time your bank offers you a cup of coffee for depositing P100,000, realize that that cup cost you P6 million.

Here's my big question: At least for your retirement fund, why not bypass the banks? Why don't you invest your money where banks invest their money?

You can. Anyone can.

Here's the table of earnings vis-à-vis interest rates.[2]

---

[2] Once again, I wish to thank the International Marketing Group who introduced me to these figures. As usual, I put stories behind the numbers.

Year	4%	8%	12%
1	100T	100T	100T
36	400T	1.6M	6.4M

For specific details of investment vehicles like bond funds, mutual funds, equity funds and stocks, I want you to do your own research. Check out **www.icap.com.ph** for a listing of mutual funds in the Philippines. If you get stumped and don't know where to go, you can email me at **bosanchez@kerygmafamily.com** for more specific information and guidance.

Don't put your retirement fund in the bank.

CHAPTER 37

Read, Listen and Practice

We are not taught financial literacy in school. It takes a lot of work and time to change your thinking and to become financially literate.
— Robert Kiyosaki

How do you gain financial literacy?

1. Read Books and Attend Seminars on Money

I strongly recommend *Think Rich, Pinoy!* and *Grow Rich, Pinoy!* both written by my financial mentor, Larry Gamboa. I recommend *Rich Dad, Poor Dad* by Robert Kiyosaki, *Millionaire Next Door* by Thomas Stanley, *Multiple Income Streams* by Robert Allen, and the other books I placed in my references at the back of this book.

Larry Gamboa also gives a Think Rich Pinoy Seminar, and I give seminars on How to Become Truly Rich (see page 205).

2. Read the Business Section of the Newspaper

I know. I used to skim through the headlines and go straight to the comics and movie section. I never opened the business section. Big mistake.

Starting today, read *every article* in that section. Yep, even if you don't understand 90 percent of what you're reading. Underline words you don't know — cashflow, portfolio, dividends, bull market, mortgage — and ask!

3. Volunteer in a Small Business

This may be my most important suggestion. There's nothing like hands-on training! Instead of watching TV or playing with videogames during weekends, work at an export company, a retail store, a hardware, a trading firm. Tell them they don't have to pay you! Just help around. But by working there, you'll learn a ton of stuff you won't learn elsewhere.

4. Get Financial Mentors

I mentioned this already but this is so important, I'll say it again here. Look for people who are successful financially. Call them up. Ask them if you could treat them out for lunch. (Take them to a park and bring two sandwiches in a brown bag.) At that lunch, ask how they became rich. Ask their secrets to success. Finally, ask them if they can teach you some more by taking you into their businesses and learning the ropes.

5. Start Your Small Business on the Side

I recommend that you start a small business. Sell sandwiches, sell lemonade, sell cell phone cards, sell anything! Or organize a concert, invest in a candy machine, rent out stuff... And don't worry if you fail the first time. And the second time. And the third time. Because what's important now is what you learn — not what you earn. Just keep on trying!

Read, listen and practice.

> Truly Rich Principle:
> **The greatest income reducer in your life right now may be your TV set.**

6 SECRET

Ride Something to Wealth

Rise early, work hard and strike oil!
— J. Paul Getty

Today, I'm taking a break with my family.

I'm writing this chapter in the cool mountains of Baguio — the Philippines' summer capital. It's 250 kilometers from Manila.

Here's my question: If you're living in Manila, can you walk up to the mountains of Baguio? Of course you can. It may take a while, but you can do it.

The average walking pace for normal human beings who don't exercise much is five kilometers an hour. (According to my friend, the only exercise he does is "carry a grudge, push his luck and jump to conclusions.") That means, it'll take 50 hours of non-stop walking to reach Baguio. If you stop for food, rest and sleep, you could probably walk for 10 hours a day. So in total, you can walk up to Baguio in five days. Not bad, right? I can't guarantee what will happen to your lungs after walking side-by-side with smoke-belching buses for five days, but at least, you'll arrive.

But you can ride a bicycle to Baguio, too.

Even if you're not a super biker, you could still pedal your way up in two days. Now that's a great improvement.

But you can improve that even further.

You can ride an air-conditioned car and arrive in five hours.

Isn't that fantastic?

And if you're really in a hurry, you can ride a plane and do it in 45 minutes.

Which is what I did this morning. I actually came from Iloilo, flew to the Manila airport — walked from the "Arrival" area to the "Departure" area — and took another plane to Baguio. And in 45 minutes, I was here. No hassle.

Friends, in the same way that there are many ways to Baguio, there are also many ways to wealth.

My rule is simple: You've got to ride something.

Remember the three kinds of people in the world?

Spenders, Savers and Investors.

Spenders don't even try to walk to their wealth. They just stay put.

Savers walk to their wealth. Yes, many people are not riding anything towards their wealth. They're just walking towards it — and that's a pity. These people are working very hard, simplifying their life, saving as much money as they can — but they put their savings *in the wrong places*. After 50 years of working hard, they look at their total net worth and it has barely grown. Some of these people retire with nothing at all. Some are a bit wiser and are able to retire owning their homes, but have nothing else. Can they feed themselves with their homes? Do their homes give them income each month? No, they don't.

The third type of person, the Investor, rides bicycles, cars and planes to his wealth.

He uses his savings and grow it exponentially.

He uses his core gifts for side business.

He uses his mentors, networks and family.

Ride *something* to wealth.

CHAPTER 38

Ride as Many Vehicles as You Can

Give portions to seven, yes to eight, for you do not know what disaster may come upon the land. Divide your portion to seven, or even to eight, for you do not know what misfortune may occur on the earth.
— Ecclesiastes 11:2

During my father's time, it was perfectly okay to have only one source of income.

My dad stayed in his company for 40 years and did pretty well. He rose from filing clerk to assistant vice president.

But times have changed. Today, it's risky to depend on your job alone.

People think it's scary to dabble with investments or to run businesses.

Let me tell you what's scary: when you only have one source of income.

Today, in a blink of an eye, many companies reorganize and fire their employees.

Today, many companies are bought, merged or simply shut down.

Now, that's scary.

You need to have many sources of income — so that if one fails, the others can sustain you.

As Robert Kiyosaki would say, financial freedom means owning many assets (paper assets, business assets and property assets) that put money in your pocket. More specifically, passive income, or income that you earn while you sleep or do something else.

Right now, I have 16 sources of income, many of them passive.

I've invested small amounts in different bonds, mutual funds, equity funds, and stocks. I've also invested in small businesses and low-cost real estate.

Each of these income streams aren't big, and you'll probably laugh at some of them. But add them together and I get a sizeable chunk each month for my needs and the needs of my ministry.

So here's the key: Don't ride one vehicle. Ride as many as you can.

Ride the bicycle. Ride the car. And ride the plane.

Correction: Ride many bicycles. Ride many cars. And ride many planes.

Even during the time of the Bible, wealthy men like Abraham, Isaac, and Job had multiple income streams.

> *And the Lord blessed the latter days of Job more than his beginning; and he had fourteen thousand sheep, six thousand camels, a thousand yoke of oxen, and a thousand she-asses.*
>
> — Job 42:12

Ride as many vehicles as you can.

Truly Rich Principle:
If you want to be rich, you need to create multiple income streams.

CHAPTER 39

Ride Your Magic "Bicycles" to Wealth

Wealth hastily gotten will dwindle, but he who gathers little by little will increase it.
— Proverbs 13:11

Let me give you an illustration on how money grows.

When I give my talks, I use an equation from Robert Allen's book, *Multiple Income Streams*. I ask people to get a P50 bill from their wallets and to look at it for a while.

I then ask, "Do you know that within that P50 bill is P50 million?"

My audience will chuckle, waiting for my punch line.

But all the more I say, "I'm not kidding. Within that P50 bill that you're holding now is P50 million!" my audience gets curious and becomes very quiet.

So I explain...

1. If you leave your P50 in your wallet, it will never grow to P50 million. The P50 million gets locked in there forever. That P50 will remain P50 even after 1,000 years. But do you know that some people actually do this? They never invest their wealth. They're like our grandmothers who placed money in the bamboo post of their nipa huts.

2. If you deposit your P50 in a special savings account that gives you three percent interest, it will grow to P50 million in 468 years. Now, I know that seems forever. But just think: Your great-great-great-great-great-great-great-great-great-great grandchild will be wealthy. Or depending on the inflation, maybe that'll be the price of a burger.

3. If you put your P50 in a bank's time deposit that gives you five percent interest, it will grow to P50 million in 284 years. I heard that they're experimenting with some new genetic procedures. If you can take some youth hormones and extend your life, you could live until you're 300 years old. But I heard that it has one side effect. Even if you're 16, you'll already look 300 years old.

4. If you put your P50 in a bond fund or mutual fund that gives you 10 percent, it will grow to P50 million in 145 years. Hey, don't laugh. My wife's grandmother is now 101 years old. So if she can only survive a few more years...

Listen. We're just talking of one measly, tiny, small, ordinary P50 bill.

The point I'm driving at is that the seed of one tiny P50 bill just needs the *right soil* and *enough time* to produce P50 million.

That's how all money works.

Can I ask you a question? How many times have you "thrown away" P50 without much thought? You spent it at something completely unnecessary.

Well, now you know you threw away P50 million.

But hey, I'm sure you have more than P50 to invest, right?

How about investing P50 a day on a mutual fund that gives 12 percent interest a year? Can you do that?

What happens if you do?

In 35 years, you'll have — drum roll please — P10 million.

That to me is riding your bicycle to wealth.

To me, bicycles are *investment funds* that grow at a higher rate than the usual inflation rate of seven percent in our country. Anything that grows at nine percent to 12 percent per year is a bicycle to wealth. (In my book, if you're growing at seven percent or less, you're *walking* towards wealth. And if you're not saving at all, you're sitting down and twiddling your thumbs.)

All of us should have the major part of our retirement fund riding bicycles. Even if you already have your own business, it's important to stash away at least 20 percent of your personal earnings from your business to these investment funds.

Why? Because business reversals and business failure can happen. So having your money growing on its own on a separate vehicle is crucial.

But understand this magic: At the later part of your investing years, the bicycle transforms into a plane.

You want proof?

Go back to my example a while ago: If you invest your P50 a day in a fund that grows at 12 percent, it will take 35 years for your money to become P10 million. But do you know how long it will take to double that figure so it becomes P20 million? Just six years more. No joke. That's how magical this bicycle is.

So don't look down on the lowly bicycle.

It's not as fast at the start but it's passive and almost non-thinking. You plop in your little money each month and see it grow as the years go by. And the magic happens.

I want you now to get off your butt and start doing some research. Ask around about bond funds, mutual funds and equity funds. And start depositing your money, not next year, or next month, but today!

Ride your magic "bicycles" to wealth.

CHAPTER 40

Ride Your "Car" to Wealth

Do what you love, the money will follow.
— Marsha Sinetar

How much did you earn last year?

Tom Cruise earned $67 million.

Tiger Woods earned $90 million.

Rock group U2 earned $110 million.

And Oprah Winfrey earned $225 million.

After reading this list, people get the false idea that to become rich, you need to be a celebrity superstar.

Not true.

All the celebrities combined — top divas, super athletes and box-office actors comprise less than one percent of all the millionaires in the world. Ninety-nine percent of the world's millionaires aren't stars at all.

Out of all the millionaires of the world...

- 1 percent are top celebrity stars — singers, actors, athletes
- 5 percent are top salesmen
- 10 percent are top specialists like doctors and lawyers
- 10 percent are top executives of mega corporations
- And 74 percent are entrepreneurs.

Most of these entrepreneurs aren't celebrities. Some of them sing like a screeching tire. Some dance like a three-day-old corpse. Some of them are terribly unathletic, they can't even win in the Special Olympics for the comatose. And some are downright ugly, even their mother faints at the sight of them.

But they're millionaires because they run businesses as diverse as selling diamonds to cleaning toilets.

My point here?

That you don't have to look like Cameron Diaz or Piolo Pascual and have the voice of Celine Dion or Regine Velasquez to become wealthy.

According to statistics, the most common way people become millionaires is by becoming a business owner.

But do you know what's common between successful stars and successful entrepreneurs?

They both use their core gift. And they have incredible passion for what they do. And this to me is the "car" towards wealth: using your core gift with passion in your own business.

A successful entrepreneur may not know how to act like Tom Cruise, or play like Tiger Woods. But I believe that every successful entrepreneur out there is like Tom Cruise and Tiger Woods because he's using his core gift to the hilt. He's in his "zone." He's doing what he was born to do.

What were you born to do?

In the next chapter, I'll discuss how to earn from your core gift.

Note: You might be wondering what riding a plane means for me. In my perspective, it's when a business becomes big business and when an investment becomes a big investment. In the meantime...

Ride your car to wealth.

Truly Rich Principle:
If you want to be rich, use your core gift with passion.

Chapter 41

Earn from Your Core Gift

Success follows doing what you want to do.
There is no other way to be successful.
— Malcolm Forbes

I have very few talents.

I don't know how to cook, how to dance, how to write a computer program and how to solve the Rubix cube. I don't know how to do geometry, trigonometry and calculus. I'm totally lost in chemistry, physics and biology. I also can't fix a leaking faucet, or do carpentry, or repair my car.

But this is what I can do very well: Communicate.

So I focus my entire life on that one thing.

I write well, and I speak well. Period.

And I delegate everything else to people who are better than I am.

The first question you need to answer is this: What is your core gift?

I have a general rule I follow in my life: I don't like complicating things just to impress you. So instead of giving you 329 psychological questions filled with scientific babble to discover your core gift (so I could impress you on how intelligent I am), let me just boil it down to two very simple questions. Stop reading this book until you answered both of these questions.

1. What do you enjoy doing?

____

____

2. What are you good at?[1]

____

____

For some of you, it's technology.
For some of you, it's teaching.
For some of you, it's selling stuff.
For some of you, it's cooking.
For some of you, it's music.
For some of you, it's advanced trigonometry. (Yes, I've heard there are such strange creatures walking on the face of the earth.)

But friend, it's not enough to discover your core gift.

You also have to ask yourself another question: How can I earn from it?

Earn from your core gift.

[1] I got these questions from the very practical, very brilliant writer Robert Ringer.

CHAPTER 42

Get Paid

Ask and you shall receive....
— Matthew 7:7

Earning from your core gift means asking to be paid.

Let me give you my story.

For the longest time, I knew that my core gift was speaking and writing — but I never really thought of earning from these gifts. I used them primarily for service. So I was content with receiving a small allowance that my organization was giving me.

So when I decided to earn more money, I tried my hand at other types of businesses. One after another, I opened a fishball kiosk on a sidewalk, a hotdog stand in a mall and a clothes store in a flea market. I also did some networking selling herbal drink, engine oil and memorial plans. (Yes, memorial plans!) Some of these earned very well for a while. But after a few months to a year, all ended up dead on the water. I couldn't understand why I kept failing. Was business this impossible?

Until it hit me: I was getting into things outside my core gifts.

It was all unfamiliar territory. Food retail? Engine oil? Memorial plans? What was I doing?

The learning curve was simply too steep. I didn't know much about these areas, it just took too long for me to learn, and while I was learning, I was losing money *fast.*

And I obviously didn't have passion for what I was doing — or I would have stuck with the business until I succeeded.

Finally, I woke up to reality and decided to stick to my core gift: Helping people live a more abundant life by my speaking and writing.

But as I said, I hit a wall: I've always done them for free — speaking in parishes, prayer groups, etcetera. Could I actually *charge* for my speaking?

Obviously, I wouldn't charge parish churches and prayer groups.

But how about companies, schools and huge organizations?

During that time, they were already asking me to speak and give seminars. And whenever they asked the question, "How much do you charge?" I turned red as a tomato, chuckled nervously, fumbled with my words and whispered beneath my breath, "Oh, I don't charge."

I was simply ashamed to ask.

Because I didn't want people to think ill of me. I didn't want people to say, "Bo has become greedy. You've got to pay him now for him to talk."

So I didn't charge.

Again and again, I'd find myself speaking to these corporate conferences in five-star hotels where everyone gets paid: the hotel, the lights and sounds, the events coordinator, even the emcee they hired for the day. Except the keynote speaker: Me. All because I didn't charge.

One day, I was invited to speak at a huge company event.

Again, they asked me how much my fee was, and again, I said, "Oh, I don't charge."

In a beautiful lush garden setting with a gigantic wooden chandelier on top, I gave my talk. After my speech, a popular singer came up the stage. I sat with the audience to enjoy the show. The man beside me was the events coordinator, and he whispered, "Bo, do you know how much we paid this singer to sing three songs? P100,000."

Wow. And how much did I get for giving my one-hour talk?

Let's just say it was enough to pay for my gas to go to their event — and buy a sandwich along the way just in case I got hungry.

All because I wasn't asking!

So one day, I decided to ask. I wrote down my speaker's fee on a piece of paper and faxed it out whenever I get invited by companies, schools and organizations. (With great pleasure, I still give my talks for free for prayer groups, parishes, prisons, etc.)

Because of this decision to ask, I now get paid well — more than enough to share with the various foundations that I run — our media ministry, our work for the poorest of the poor, our counseling center, etc.

Today, I also formed the most dynamic, effective speakers in the Philippines to be corporate trainors for Beaconlight, our training organization. We help companies train their leaders, change their culture, and increase their productivity through our unique training courses.

Because of my spiritual background, our seminars and courses help develop enduring character values in their employees, not just faddish corporate slogans. It also has a spiritual angle not found in other training programs. Instead of hiding this spiritual component to make it more appealing, we actually make it our USP or unique selling proposition. Now, companies want us because we have a spiritual angle in our courses.[1]

I'm able to do what I love to do — and earn at the same time.

Get paid.

[1] For more information, please call BEACONLIGHT at (+632) 722-9562 or email beaconlightevents@gmail.com

CHAPTER 43

Learn to Sell

You can have everything you want if you help enough people get what they want.
— Zig Ziglar

If you're serious in starting a business, get a sales job.

Sell something!

Sell insurance, jewellery, cars, cookware, clothes, vacuum cleaners.

It'll train your personality, remove shyness from your system and help you face your fears. It'll kick you out of your comfort zone and make you do things you've never done before. It'll train you to make that phone call, knock on doors, and get rejected again and again and again until it doesn't hurt anymore. (I'm lying. It will always hurt.)

You've got to eat rejection for breakfast, lunch and dinner. But there's nothing like selling that will make you ready for starting a business.

Because any business means selling something — whether it's a product or a service.

Always remember that selling means you want to meet a person's need.

So what do you call that? You're serving someone.

Let me get mushy: You're loving the customer.

That should be the reason for selling — aside from earning money.

Which brings me to networking or multi-level marketing (MLM).

Some people claim it's the next best thing to heaven. Others claim it was invented by the devil himself. Some believe it's God's gift to mankind. Others believe it's a curse that destroys friendships, families and our spiritual lives.

Sorry, both views aren't quite right.

Like anything else in the world, MLM can be a blessing or a curse, depending on who actually does it.

In the previous chapter, I told you that I sold herbal drinks, engine oil and memorial plans. That didn't last long but I earned a lot of money selling stuff.

But my real profit wasn't money.

It was the enormous skills and financial education I developed — how to recruit, how to motivate, how to train, how to sell, how to control costs, how to sell.... Skills that I would need in my future businesses.

Learn how to sell.

Truly Rich Principle:
Your first profit in any business is financial wisdom, not money.

CHAPTER 44

Remember That Profits Are Better Than Wages

Wages make you a living;
Profits make you a fortune.
— Jim Rohn

Most schools are teaching kids to be employees.

And employees don't need to learn much about money. Because they get their salary each month in a nice little envelope or get it deposited directly into their ATM account.

Nice arrangement, really. Just do what you're told — clean the floor, or sell the stuff, or pull a tooth, or cook the food, or build the bridge — and you'll receive a regular paycheck each month.

Consequently, we've become a country of employees.[1]

Unless we become a country of *entrepreneurs*, our country will never prosper.

Or unless we start having an *entrepreneur's* mindset.

Don't think I'm asking all of you to start businesses.

Even if you remain an employee for life, you won't go up the ranks until you have an entrepreneur's mind.

Listen to what Filipino parents tell their kids: *"Study hard so you can get a good job."* Now listen to what Filipino-Chinese parents tell their kids: *"Study hard so you can have a good business."*

As early as six years old, a Chinese kid is helping his father in the family hardware, bakery, grocery or funeral parlor. The little boy learns how to buy cheap, sell profitably, maintain a small inventory, monitor cashflow and negotiate with clients.

[1] But some say that this is good. Because we're migrating globally to become the world's best employees. We have become the world's best nannies, seamen, caregivers, nurses, teachers and computer programmers. Is that good? Not necessarily. At best, I want to see migration as a temporary solution.

Remember this principle: *Profits are always better than wages.*

Wages — or salaries — come regularly, and people are content with that.

But that's as far as they go. If you get an increase, if you get promoted, it goes up by 10 percent, perhaps 20 percent....

But in your investments and businesses, *you* determine your profits.

Do you want a 100 percent increase next year? Decide.

Do you want a 1,000 percent increase in five years? Decide.

It's really all up to you.

Sure, that would mean growing *yourself* so that you could grow your investments and businesses, by borrowing money, by expanding, by putting up other branches, by franchising, by selling your business and starting a new one....

But the point is — you decide.

I repeat: If you can't handle the growth of the business, then grow as a person first. When you've grown enough, then start growing your business. (In the next chapter, I'll talk more about this growth.)

Hold on to your full-time job, but start thinking like an entrepreneur.

Be an investor and start something on the side.

Remember that profits are better than wages.

Truly Rich Principle:
If you want to be rich, develop an entrepreneur mindset — even if you're an employee.

CHAPTER 45

Expand Your Territories

Everything you want is just outside your comfort zone.
— Robert Allen

Many people ask me how I'm able to do all that I do.

Let me give you an idea of my responsibilities. (Warning: Some people actually get tired just reading this list, so take a deep breath...)

I lead four non-profit organizations. I speak in a daily radio program, a daily Internet reality show and a weekly TV program. Each year, I churn out three books, produce four audio/video teaching series, and write more than 200 articles. I publish six magazines, maintain four websites, send out my online newsletter and write my blog. I lead a "virtual" community called the Kerygma Family and oversee an incredible "sales force" called the Kerygma Ambassadors. I also travel extensively, preaching 300 plus times a year all over the Philippines and around the world — leading retreats, seminars and prayer rallies. I also am proud to say that I read all my email — and answer 75 percent of them.

As if these aren't enough, there are a "few" personal things that I do...

I own a homeschool center called the Catholic Filipino Academy that teaches parents how to homeschool their kids. I lead a financial consultancy organization to teach Filipinos how to save for their future. I run a tiny organic farm, a real estate business, and manage a few more small businesses. (Plus, my seven-year-old boy still has his *bangus* business, and he's hired me to be his marketing consultant.)

Of course, I'm fanatical about spending time with my family. I play with my sons every day and still take my beautiful wife once a week on a romantic date. We also have four family vacations every year, and two of those vacations are two-week long trips!

And each year, I read three books a week, listen to the same number of audio books, not to mention the thousands of magazine and Internet articles I read.

Oh, before I forget, let me mention that I hop on a stationary bike one hour a day.

How do I do all these things?

First, I believe God has given us more capacity than we think we have.

The ultimate crime is that we belittle ourselves.

We think we're insects, so we live an insect life, but actually — we're giants!

Because of this, I believe you can earn 10 times more than whatever you're earning right now. (It will take some time of course to work it out through wise investing, but it's possible.) You can help 10 times the number of people you're helping now.

Don't limit yourself.

You're bigger than you think you are.

Second, I believe that love is limitless. It has no boundaries.

I do what I do because I want to love people.

Each morning, I wake up and ask myself, "How can I bless people today?"

And so I stretch. I go just a teensy bit beyond what I *think* is my limit — and my capacities expand — because I want to bless the world.

Third, I build my Dream Team.

Fourth, I create an auto pilot system.

I'll discuss these last two items in the next two chapters.

Expand your territories.

Truly Rich Principle:
Wake up each morning and ask, "How can I bless the world more?"

CHAPTER 46

Create Passive Income

Not all businesses are created equal.

Some businesses are just glorified jobs.

Let me tell you the story of Maria.

Maria was an accountant in a huge company. She had so much work, she worked until late into the evening every single night. Obviously, she hated her job. She felt trapped in her 8 a.m. to 10 p.m. prison every day.

One day, she walked into a bookstore. On impulse, she bought a book on how to start a business. She read it in one sitting and got all revved up. Maria began to dream of having her own *carinderia.*[1]

You see, Maria loved to cook. As a child, Maria was a helper in grandma's canteen. Through her mentor, she learned how to market, how to create delicious meals, how to run a kitchen like a battleship and how to make customers happy.

Maria resigned from her job and jumped headlong into her new business.

And people loved her food. And because her house was on a busy street, sales were brisk and profits were good.

Maria was having the time of her life. She was doing what she loved and was earning more than her accountant's salary.

There was just one problem: One year into the business, Maria realized she was working *harder* and *longer* than when she was an accountant. Yes, she still worked until 10 in the evening. But this time, she didn't start at 8 a.m. but at 4 a.m., because she had to do the marketing early in the morning. It was an 18-hour job.

Sure, she loved what she was doing. It was clearly her core gift and passion. But would she be able to continue with this backbreaking schedule?

[1] Simple eatery

From my point of view, Maria replaced one job with another job. Yes, the second job is now her own, but unless she *trains* others to do her work and *duplicates* herself, it's just a glorified job. Unless she changes her approach, she will suffer from two things:

1. Entrepreneur's Burnout

Maria is a perfectionist and can't delegate. She can't see someone else in front of her stove (she calls it her throne). She believes she has to be the one who does the cooking or the food wouldn't taste the same. When a business owner is like Maria, burnout isn't far away. Stress will build up until Maria gets sick physically or emotionally — and may be forced to give up the business.

2. Dead-End Profits

Maria can never expand her business and increase her profit exponentially. Her earnings will remain stuck. Or if ever it will increase, it will increase via addition, not multiplication.

Remember that one of your goals is passive income.

You need to set up the business in such a way that, one day, it can run without you. Or at least, with minimal supervision. Your goal is that while you sleep, your business earns for you.

When Maria can train cooks to duplicate her culinary skills and managers to duplicate her managing skills, she can exponentially expand her income by doing any of the following: offer catering services for parties, or start a new branch in another part of the city, or sell her sauces in bottles, or write cookbooks, or start her own cooking show on TV!

That's why every time I enter into any project, I always do it with a team around me. Never alone.

And together, we create a system for the project that's replicable and duplicable.

In other words, it's got to run on autopilot without my direct supervision.

Here's my ideal leader: If I appoint someone to be project head (or organization director or business manager), *after six months,* I don't want her bothering me anymore except for major directional issues. If she still bothers me for tiny matters, I've chosen the wrong leader — or I trained her wrongly.

Create passive income.

Truly Rich Principle:
If you want to be rich, you need to create a system that is replicable.

CHAPTER 47

Earn Exponential Income

And other seeds fell into good soil and brought forth grain, growing up and increasing and yielding thirtyfold and sixtyfold and a hundredfold.
— Mark 4:8

Henry Hungry is applying for a job.

He walks into this nice office and meets a well-dressed fellow behind the desk. Henry smiles and asks him, "Sir, is there a job here for me?"

The man says, "I'm actually looking for a general manager. You need to sign a contract for three years. Interested?"

"Hmm. Sorry for being upfront, but how much will I earn?" Henry Hungry asks.

The man says, "I'll let you choose your salary. Do you want P30,000 a month or one centavo doubled every month?"

Henry Hungry is mildly shocked by this unorthodox offer. "Run that by me again please," he says, getting his cell phone to calculate.

The man chuckles. "Option 1 is I pay you P30,000 a month for 36 months. Option 2 is I pay you one centavo on the first month and I double it every month for 36 months."

Henry starts calculating. "Option 2 is interesting. If I choose that, I earn one centavo on the first month, two centavos on the second month, four centavos on the third month, eight centavos on the fourth month, 16 centavos on the fifth month, 32 centavos on the sixth month... after 12 months of working with you, I would have received a total of... sheesh, P23! Sir, I need the money badly. I choose Option 1 where I earn P30,000 flat each month. By the first year, I'd already have earned P360,000. And after three years, that would total to P1 million. I definitely choose Option 1."

"Okay, if that's what you want." Then the man asks, "By the way, if you chose Option 2, do you know how much you'll earn by the end of three years?"

"I didn't finishing computing that option. It's too depressing."

The man calculates in front of Henry Hungry. "On the first month, you receive one centavo, on the second month, you receive two centavos...." He goes on and on, and Henry doesn't mind him too much. He's too focused on the P1 million he'll be earning in three years. He feels pretty good about himself.

Finally, the man looks up and shows Henry Hungry the calculator. "In 36 months, you would have earned P680 Million. You exchanged that for one million. I'm sorry, my friend, I can't take you as my general manager. Your decision-making skills are terrible."

Let me give you the figures...

Months	Option #1	Option #2
1	P30,000	1 centavo
2	P30,000	2 centavos
3	P30,000	4 centavos
4	P30,000	8 centavos
5	P30,000	16 centavos
6	P30,000	32 centavos
7	P30,000	64 centavos
8	P30,000	P1.28
9	P30,000	P2.56
10	P30,000	P5.12
11	P30,000	P10.24
12	P30,000	P20.48
13	P30,000	P40.96
14	P30,000	P81.92
15	P30,000	P163.84
16	P30,000	P327.68
17	P30,000	P655.36
18	P30,000	P1,310.72
19	P30,000	P2,621.44
20	P30,000	P5,242.88
21	P30,000	P10,485.76
22	P30,000	P20,971.52
23	P30,000	P41,943.04
24	P30,000	P83,886.08
25	P30,000	P167,772.16
26	P30,000	P335,544.32
27	P30,000	P671,088.64
28	P30,000	P1,342,177.28
29	P30,000	P2,684,354.56
30	P30,000	P5,368,709.12
31	P30,000	P10,737,418.24
32	P30,000	P21,474,836.48
33	P30,000	P42,949,672.96
34	P30,000	P85,899,345.92
35	P30,000	P171,798, 691.84
36	P30,000	P343,597,383.68
Total	**P1 million+**	**P680 million+**

Obviously, I'm using this as an analogy.

There are only two types of income in this world: *Linear* and *Exponential.*

In my fictional story above, Option 1 is *Linear* and Option 2 is *Exponential.*

Linear income is like a piece of bread. You eat it and it's gone. After that, you have to look for another piece of bread.

Exponential income is like a seed. You can't eat it at first, but if you plant it and wait for a while, you can eat as much fruit as you want to. You have an infinite source of fruit if you keep on planting some of the seeds.

Many Filipinos today have only one income stream — their jobs — and jobs are linear income.

Some Filipinos are self-employed and run small businesses. Sadly, like Maria in my example in the last chapter, these businesses are linear income, too. (For example, doctors and dentists may have their own clinics, but they still earn linear income. Unless they work, they don't earn. They've not been able to create passive income.)

What is exponential income?

That's what a regular employee earns when he invests in mutual funds and stocks. (So you see, everyone can earn exponential income, even employees.)

That's what a networker earns when she builds a downline organization.

That's what an infropreneur earns when he sells an e-book or when he earns from Google ads from his website.

That's what a sales manager earns from his salesmen.

That's what a distributor earns when he distributes his goods to various stores.

That's what a store owner earns when she branches out, hires other store managers, or sells franchises of her store.

That's what a real estate investor earns when she buys profitable rental property.

That's what an author earns when she earns a royalty for every book that's sold.

That's what a singer earns when she earns a royalty for every album sold.

That's what an inventor earns when he invents a widget and enters into a deal with a company to sell it.

That's what a dentist earns when he hires other dentists and opens new clinics.

Exponential income — also called passive income — means earning for a very long time from work you did only once at the very start.

Hey, income is income. Earn linear income when you can!

But invest your linear income so you can earn exponential income.

Because if you want to become wealthy, you need to find a way to earn exponential income.

Earn exponential income.

Truly Rich Principle:
Invest your linear income so you can earn exponential income.

CHAPTER 48

Build Your Dream Team

It takes a village to raise a child.
— African proverb

Personally, I don't think anything great is accomplished without a team.

Even Jesus had a team around Him.

A few months ago, I was reading about the interesting world of horse-pulling competitions.

That's where huge horses the size of elephants pull massive concrete blocks behind them.

Did you know that the grand champion horse could pull the incredible weight of 4,500 pounds? If the average weight of a Filipino is 140 pounds (which happens to be my weight before I eat my breakfast), that means this super horse could carry 32 Filipinos — without wheels! That monster could pull me, my wife, my kids, my parents, my siblings, their spouses, their kids, and all my in-laws combined.

And the second placer horse can pull only slightly lower than the first placer: 4,400 pounds.

That was when the organizers got curious. If these two horses pulled together, how many pounds could they carry? Could they pull 8,900 pounds?

They harnessed both horses and were shocked with the results.

Both horses, when pulling together, carried the mind-blowing weight of 12,000 pounds. That's 85 Filipinos.

My message? Teams are powerful.

Alone, I can do a lot of things. But with my team, I don't add but multiply what I can do.

As I told you, I don't enter into a project without a team around me.

And I choose my team well.

I have a very simple criteria: I choose men and women who are humble (team players) and who are experts in their field. In other words, I search for impeccable character and fantastic skills.

After many years of building my Dream Team, I've got fantastic leaders, administrators, accountants, speakers, finance wizards, computer geniuses, marketing experts, media experts, architects, etcetera.

And every day, I *constantly* expand my team.

I keep networking. I circulate. I meet people. I build bridges.

Recently, I saw a giant Dream Team around one man.

I had the privilege of speaking to the 120 top leaders of the telecom giant Globe — from CEO Jerry Ablaza to his vice presidents and senior managers.

Before my talk, Jerry Ablaza gave the vision of the company for the coming year.

I was awed by the incredible Dream Team around Jerry. It takes a special person with incredible leadership skills to lead a powerful team, and Jerry was that man. It was a gathering of the best of the best, but united, as a single force soaring its way to a vision. Man, I was inspired.

No wonder Globe is where it is today.

It has a Dream Team leading it — and a leader who knew how to pick his team and lead his team.

Build your Dream Team.

Truly Rich Principle:
Nothing great can be accomplished without a team. Even Jesus had a team.

CHAPTER 49

Market, Market and Market Some More

The only reason to be in business is to create a customer.
— Peter Drucker

"You made this?"

I was holding a tiny gold basket with little trinkets inside.

"Yes, I did," Pinky smiled with her chin raised in pride.

Pinky made novelty items. Cheap stuff from Divisoria[1] transformed into beautiful creations in her gifted hands.

"Wow, this would be very pretty wedding souvenirs," I said, "Business must be very good."

"Not really," she pouted, "orders aren't coming in."

I shook my head, "You have no problem with your products. You have a problem telling people about them."

"Oh, I'm just not that kind of a person," she said, "I'm basically an artist. I just like staying at home making these things."

I've met a lot of Pinkys among small business owners.

Many businesses fail because the business owner spends too much time perfecting her product and very little time telling people about it. Usually, the entrepreneur spends 80 percent of her time on improving her product and 20 percent on marketing her product.

Bad move. Very few businesses can survive that kind of math.

Chisel this on stone: Marketing is the lifeblood of all business. So market, market and market some more!

Because I don't care how great your product is, if people don't know about it, they won't buy it.

If you want to succeed, you need to reverse your math. *Spend 80 percent of your time in marketing and 20 percent of your time in developing your product.*

[1] Manila's cheapest market

That's why the best entrepreneurs I've seen are those who, in their early years, had selling experience. Day in and day out, they were selling stuff on the street, face to face, belly to belly, handshake to handshake.

Because every entrepreneur must have a *marketing* mindset.

And I've now realized that marketing can never be delegated by the owner to his marketing head. The marketing head is only his assistant. The owner must be the main marketing machine.

First, you must build your relationship with your existing customers.

You must constantly communicate with your customer. The customer needs to see you as a friend. Business is all about building relationships. Because if all factors are equal, I'd rather buy from a friend than a stranger.

That means communicating with your customers constantly. Through email, through snail mail, through phone calls, through gifts, through personal visits.

Market, market and market some more.

Truly Rich Principle:
Spend 80 percent of your time in marketing and 20 percent of your time in developing your product.

SECRET 7

Have a Bias for Action

You can't cross a sea by merely staring into the water.
— Rabindranath Tagore

When I was a teen, a Bible teacher once told me, "Do you know that the line, 'God helps those who help themselves' isn't in the Bible? It's not from the Lord."

"Wow, I didn't know that," I said.

He continued, "The greatest sin is the sin of self-sufficiency. That we think we can do it without God."

I was impressed by his wisdom. He said, "As Spirit-led Christians, we should depend totally on the Holy Spirit. Before my conversion, I just made my own plans and decided on my own. But today, I listen to God first."

For some people, as long as it isn't in the Bible, we shouldn't believe it.

Today, I realize that's absurd.

Is advanced trigonometry in the Bible? Are the laws of quantum physics in the Bible? Is the Dogma of the Holy Trinity (the term itself) in the Bible?

Nope. Yet we believe in them.

As long as we don't contradict the Bible, we're okay.

What does the line "God helps those who help themselves" mean?

Is it really the sin of self-sufficiency?

No. God *wants* us to help ourselves.

He doesn't want us to remain toddlers.

Like any ordinary parent, He wants us to grow up and take responsibility.

In fact, I believe God primarily moves in this world through our action.

Have a bias for action.

CHAPTER 50

Look for Natural Signs

Nothing happens unless something moves.
— Albert Einstein

How did young David defeat an eight-foot giant named Goliath?

Aside from the fact that God was with him, David had a bias for action.

As a young shepherd guarding his sheep, he fought lions and bears.

Imagine for a moment if David didn't have a bias for action.

Imagine if he were like some of us religious people — always unsure unless God sends us a sign from above.

One day, David sees the lion approaching one of his lambs.

He prays, "Oh Lord, what do you want me to do? The lion is going to eat the poor sheep. Oh, give me a sign! Let someone give me a red rose and I will attack that lion!"

Nothing happens. He doesn't see a red rose. Instead, he sees red blood squirting from a mangled little lamb.

"Oh dear, one lamb down." David says, "Lord, please speak to me and tell me what to do. I'll cut the Bible." He shuts his eyes, breaks open his Bible, points to a word, and reads, *"Wait upon the Lord..."* He looks up to the sky and says, "Okay, Lord, I'll wait."

By this time, the lion grabs a second lamb. "Oh no," David sighs. "Lord, do you want me to now go and fight the lion? Let me cut the Bible again." He does it and reads, "'*The Lord giveth and the Lord taketh away....*' Oh yes, Lord, this is a trial happening in my life — and You want me to accept this...."

I'm exaggerating, but I hope you get my point.

Some religious people act this way.

At least, I used to.

I wouldn't move until I was sure it was God's will. That was supposed to be a good thing, but I had a narrow view of what God's will was or how He revealed it to me. I expected God to speak to me through supernatural signs — a prophetic voice, signs and wonders, thunder and lightning. I didn't realize that more often, He speaks through natural signs.

In my crazy example above, David was praying for a sign from God — a red rose — when right in front of him was a natural sign — the lion itself.

Have a bias for action.

CHAPTER 51

Make Things Happen

Talent is cheaper than table salt.
What separates the talented individual from the successful one is a lot of hard work.
— Stephen King

Have you seen a little booklet called *Didache?*

For years now, *Didache* has been the most widely read daily Bible reflection guide in the Philippines. This little dynamite devotional has been blessing hundreds of thousands of people. When I published its first issue (and wrote probably 50 percent of its reflections) way back in 1994, I never thought it would be the great success that it is now.

Through the years, at different times, people have told me, "You know Bo? Before you came up with *Didache,* I already thought of coming up with something like that. I envisioned having different people write their reflections on the daily Bible readings of each day...."

When we launched *Sabbath,* another daily Bible guide where priests write one homily a day, again, a lot of people said, "Gosh, Bo, I was thinking of creating something exactly like this. I already had a list of priests who'd write for me...."

My point? My ideas aren't unique. A lot of people think of them.

But here's the difference: I just don't think of the ideas. I make the idea *happen.* And usually, I make it happen fast.

In other words, I have a bias for action.

I've used the same principle for all our other projects: our work for the poor, our radio and TV programs, our Internet TV show, our cell phone ministry....

When I think about it, I make it happen.

A lot of people use this strategy for their projects:

Ready... Aim... Fire!

I have a slightly different strategy for my projects:

Ready... Fire! Aim...

(And fire again... Aim...and fire again... Aim... and fire again...)

Hey, I'm not talking about recklessness. Remember, the first step is "Ready."

But I use this strategy because I want to avoid the very common strategy of many people:

Ready... Aim... Aim... Aim... Aim... Aim...

They just aim. They never pull the trigger.

Why? Because they want to cross every "t" and dot every "i" before they start anything. But for pioneers, perfectionism is never a good strategy.

My plan is to fail and improve along the way.

I risk failure. And I risk success.

Make things happen.

Truly Rich Principle:
For pioneers, perfectionism is never a good strategy.

Chapter 52

Fail Your Way to Success

When we give ourselves permission to fail,
we at the same time give ourselves permission to excel.
— Eloise Ristad

Do you know the difference between a successful and an unsuccessful person?

Easy: Count the number of times each person has failed. I bet you, the successful person has failed 10 times more than the unsuccessful person.

Michael Jordan is known as the greatest basketball player in the world. In the Guiness Book of World Records, Michael is on the list of players who have made the most number of baskets in the NBA.

Yet many people don't know that he's also in the Guiness list of players who've made the most misses. Because he simply made the most attempts.

> *I've missed more than 9,000 shots in my career. I've lost almost 300 games. Twenty six times, I've been trusted to take the game winning shot and missed. I've failed over and over and over again in my life. And that is why I succeed.*
>
> — Michael Jordan

Another story I like to share is Soichiro's story.

He began making piston rings. He tried selling it to Toyota but they rejected him. Business was so bad, he pawned his wife's jewelry to keep his business afloat. After building his factory, it got burned to the ground.

What did Soichiro do? He built it again.

That was when it burned down a second time.

He built it up again.

Not long after that, an earthquake tore his factory.

He built it up a third time.

Because of the war, gas was expensive. So to go around, Soichiro used his bicycle. But he attached a little engine to it so that he didn't have to pedal. When everyone who saw it wanted one, he knew he had a winner in his hands.

His full name is Soichiro Honda. He became the first mass producer of motorcycles. He says:

> *Success can be achieved only through repeated failure. My success represents the one percent of the work that resulted from the 99 percent that was called failure.*
>
> — Soichiro Honda

Fail your way to success.

Truly Rich Principle:
Do you know the difference between a successful and an unsuccessful person? The successful person has failed 10 times more than the unsuccessful person.

CHAPTER 53

Take Bold Massive Action

The bolder the action, the greater the genius, magic, and power that is likely to flow from it.
— Robert Ringer

Robert Ringer wrote a book entitled *Action* and I love it.

It's a great kick-in-the-butt for those who like to endlessly plan, dream and do nothing.

If you want to succeed in life, there's no other path: You've got to take bold, massive action.

No timid, tepid, tentative steps.

No half-baked, half-hearted actions.

Use all your guns and pull all triggers and unload all your bullets.

Fire all cylinders.

Floor the gas pedal.

Give it all you've got.

When I look back at my life, all I see are a long line of bold, massive actions that *failed*. But I didn't stop. I just kept taking more bold, massive actions until I succeeded.

The first magazine I published folded up in one year. Crashed. Fizzled. Went up in smoke and vanished forever in the cemetery of extinct publications.

But after that failure, I launched *Kerygma*. After 20 years, it still is the widest read inspirational magazine in the country.

My first book was a failure too. We printed 6,000 copies and forgot all about it. My grammar was so bad, I cringe when I read it today. Back then, if you wanted me to hide my head under the ground like an ostrich, read a portion of that book to me.

For 10 years, I forgot about book writing for a long time.

But finally, I wrote my second book and it became a bestseller.

I've written eight books so far, and every single one of them has become a national bestseller.

When I began Anawim, our work for the poorest of the poor, our first three years were three years of chaos. No, that's not quite right. They were three years of *total* chaos. We simply didn't know what we were doing.

In my desire to help the poor, I accepted everyone — orphans, abandoned elderly, deranged, drug addicts, alcoholics, street kids, ex-convicts, kidney dialysis patients.... Can you imagine the nightmare we went through during our early years? The drug addicts were teaching the orphans to take drugs, the deranged became violent (brandishing a knife and attacking my staff), and tuberculosis patients were mingling and infecting everyone else.

But after 10 years in operation, spending P400,000 a month for food, medicines and housing (God provides each month), we learned the ropes little by little and run a tight ship today.

I hear visitors tell me that Anawim is the most peaceful and calm home for the aged they've ever seen. (Visit us. Call (632) 710-5273 for more information.)

And since we began, we've already served one million meals.

Recently, I'm taking bold, massive action towards another goal: of having a TV station that will broadcast God's love through six daily inspirational TV shows.

Will it be expensive to run our own TV channel?

You bet. Probably close to P100 million.

Do I have the money? Nope.

But will God provide?

If it's His plan, He always does.

Take bold massive action.

Truly Rich Principle:
If you want to succeed, don't take timid, tepid, tentative steps. Give it all you've got.

CHAPTER 54

Apply the 10 Sacred Rules of Success

Take the first step in faith. You don't have to see the whole staircase.
— Martin Luther King, Jr.

Let me share with you my 10 Sacred Rules of Success.

I must warn you that it's very complicated. Its concepts are very deep and I'm afraid many won't understand these principles. I apologize for the obtuse terminology. Please use a dictionary if you can't understand any of the terms I use.

Here they are: (drum roll please...)

Ten Sacred Rules of Success
Rule #1: Act.
Rule #2: Act again.
Rule #3: Act again.
Rule #4: Act again.
Rule #5: Act again.
Rule #6: Act again.
Rule #7: Act again.
Rule #8: Act again.
Rule #9: Act again.
Rule #10: Act again.

I cannot overemphasize this principle: Allow yourself to fail.

And when you do, forgive yourself. And act again.

Never label anyone (yourself included) a failure.

The dreaded Yakuza members cut off their fingers whenever they failed in an assignment. They get a sharp knife, wrap their little finger with a handkerchief so the blood won't spurt, and slice it off. What a terrible thing to do! Because for the rest of their lives, they'll look at their hand and remind themselves of their failure.

Some people I know aren't Yakuza members but they do the same thing. They *cut* a part of their lives and label themselves failures forever. They subconsciously punish themselves by losing a relationship, or losing their health by getting sick, or losing their spiritual life because they don't believe God can forgive them.

Instead of spending your energies on condemning yourself, spend it on acting again and trying one more time.

Remember General Douglas McArthur? He applied at West Point, was rejected, applied again, was rejected a second time, and applied for the third time! In time, he became one of the greatest generals of World War II.

Have you ever read *Chicken Soup for the Soul* by Jack Canfield and Mark Hanson? After writing the book, no one wanted to publish it. The authors approached 33 publishers in New York and 90 publishers in California—and every single publisher rejected them. But they never gave up. Finally, a small publisher accepted their book. It went on to sell 53 million copies.

Apply the 10 sacred rules of success.

Truly Rich Principle:
Allow yourself to fail.

CHAPTER 55

Hustle

The secret to my success is that I bit off more than I could chew and chewed as fast as I could.
— Paul Hogan

There are over 7.5 millionaires in America today.

Around 20 percent of those millionaires are high school grads only.

There are 222 billionaires in America, and a full 10 percent are college dropouts.

Why mention these facts?

Because I hear a lot of people say, "I'll never make it in life. I don't have a college degree." Go tell that to Bill Gates, the richest man in the world. Because he never finished college, too.

I'm not saying education isn't important.

It's very important.

But if you want to succeed in life (in any area of life actually) — education isn't enough. You need something else…

I call it the Power of Hustle.

Hustle can mean something bad. In today's jargon, "He's a hustler," means he's a cheat. I'm *not* using that definition here.

I'm using that word the way they use it in basketball.

When the coach shouts, "Hustle, boys!" he's telling them to run fast, think on their feet, be aggressive and defend like a maniac. *To hustle means to believe that there's a solution to almost any problem — and to take it upon yourself to find it!*

I've seen the Power of Hustle in the most successful human beings in the world.

They know what they want. They take responsibility. They keep on moving. And they never take "no" for an answer.

Mother Teresa had it.

Sam Walton had it.

Steve Jobs has it.

Bill Gates has it.

Nanay Coring has it.

I had the great pleasure of meeting *Nanay* Coring or Socorro Ramos, founder of National Bookstore. At 83 years old, you'd think she was 50. I felt her sense of wonder, her vibrancy and love for life.

To me, *Nanay* Coring embodied the power of hustle, a *never-say-die* attitude towards life.

On a busy sidewalk, she propped up a tiny table, piled some books on top, and called it National Bookstore. What do you call that? I call that hustle.

War broke out and the Japanese censored all books sold, effectively prohibiting her from selling books.

Did she give up? No. She hustled. She looked for what people needed — and discovered that the Japanese soldiers wore boots the whole day. Would they need slippers? In time, she sold thousands of rubber slippers to them at her "bookstore."

One day, one of these Japanese officials asked if she was selling bond paper. When she asked how many he needed, he shocked her by saying, "Three thousand reams." (She later learned that he was in charge of printing Japanese money.) At that point, she didn't have a single piece of bond paper with her. But with courage, she said, "I'll deliver 3,000 reams to you."

She looked far and near, buying bond paper with her *kalesa*, delivering it to them on time.

That's hustle.

By that time, her house was filled with piles of Japanese money — soon to be worthless if the Americans won. And listening to short-wave radio at home, she knew this was going to happen soon.

That was when a Japanese sold her a whole warehouse of whisky. She bargained and bargained, giving him all her Japanese money. When the Americans won the war, she displayed the whisky on the sidewalk — and the American soldiers bought them with US dollars.

When the war ended, things were looking up. She expanded and made good profit.

And then a storm blew away their roof, and the rain drenched all their books. In one night, everything she earned the past years was all wiped out.

Did *Nanay* Coring give up? No. She hustled.

She started from zero and built NBS one book at a time, one customer at a time.

She calls herself a simple saleslady.

And she will always be the best saleslady on the floor.

Today, National Bookstore or NBS is the widest bookstore chain in the Philippines with 85 branches scattered all over the country. Aside from NBS, *Nanay* Coring now also owns other huge companies.

Luck?

No.

Hustle.

Truly Rich Principle:
To hustle means to believe that there's a solution to almost any problem — and to take it upon yourself to find it!

8 SECRET

Win in All Areas

Delight yourself in the Lord and
He shall give you the desires of your heart.
Psalms 37:4

My priest-friend told me this story.

He said that one day, in his parish, he saw a couple with their 12-year-old boy. He approached the mother and said, "Pray that your son becomes a priest."

The mother was shocked, held her son in a protective embrace, and said, "Father, not this one. He's good-looking!"

The priest raised his eyebrow. "Do you mean to tell me that all priests are ugly?"

Many people have certain stereotypes of spiritual people: that they have to be ugly, poor and pathetic.

This is absolutely nuts.

A spiritual person can be handsome, rich and happy.

In other words, we can win in all areas of life.

Because it's useless to win in one area and be defeated in another.

What's the use of having millions when your family is in shambles?

What's the use of being physically healthy when your spiritual life is empty?

You need balance.

You need to win in the seven major areas of life.

You need to:

1. Strengthen Your Relationships
2. Grow in Emotional Maturity
3. Use Your Core Gift
4. Get Physically Healthy
5. Gain Wisdom
6. Build Your Money
7. Nourish Your Spiritual Life

Is it possible?

I believe in the power of our beliefs to define our reality.

If you believe that it's not possible to win in all areas, then you won't be able to do it. But if you believe at the core of your being that it's possible, then it is.

Win in all areas of life.

CHAPTER 56

Follow Your Inner Compass

If you miss love, you miss life.
— Leo Buscaglia

I write with passion.

When I write, I'm so focused, I get lost in a different world.

That's why every time my son enters my home office and asks, "Daddy, can you play with me?" I get agitated. It's like I'm driving a race car at 200 kph and someone spikes my tires to shreds — and I hear the deafening sound of metal on gravel.

And each time, I take a deep breath, and ask my inner compass, "What is my highest value? *Efficiency or love*?"

And like being hit by a 10-foot wave, my irritation is swept away.

I look at the expectant eyes of my son and ask him, "What do you want to play?" He takes my hand and leads me to his room. We sit on the floor and build castles, bridges and towers with wooden blocks — all the time talking, laughing and singing.

Man, I have the greatest time in my life.

And I almost missed it if it were not for my inner compass.

What is the inner compass anyway?

When you're lost in a jungle, you need a compass.

Because the compass — no matter how you shake it, twirl it, spin it, flip it — will always point to north, it can guide you through your journey.

Stephen Covey says your most important values are like your inner compass pointing to your most important and highest values. For me, my inner compass is God's voice in my soul. Some also call it their conscience.

Here's the truth: In the end, long-term happiness can only come from consistently living by our inner compass.

Why? Because our beings were designed to follow love.

One day, President Ramon Magsaysay was complaining about why sugar prices were down. His economist told him, "Well, sir, we can't do anything about it. It's the law of supply and demand."

Magsaysay got angry and said, "Who made that law? I'm the President of the Republic! *Repeal that law!*"

An awkward silence hung in the air. People looked at each other, wondering who would have the courage to correct the President.

Finally, one guy had the courage to say, "Sir, the law of supply and demand is like the law of gravity. We cannot repeal that, sir."

At that, the President threw his fist on the table and said, "I'm the President! I repeal the law of gravity!"

Friends, your inner compass is based on natural, universal laws that's like the law of gravity. They too can never be repealed.

The Law of Love, the Law of Forgiveness, the Law on Justice, the Law of Holiness, the Law of Purity.... These are absolute laws! They can never be changed. If we don't follow them, we destroy ourselves.

Follow your inner conscience.

Truly Rich Principle:
My inner compass is God's voice in my soul.

CHAPTER 57

Define Your Own Success

Poverty is a state of mind often induced by looking at a neighbor's car.
— Anonymous

I loved my old car.

Even if it was nine years old.

It had traveled over 200,000 kilometers in my trips, bringing me to the farthest corners of Luzon. In one sense, he was my traveling buddy — and a faithful one, too.

Not once had he failed me in a major way.

Sometimes, I think I was crazy. Because when I rode it, I even tapped its dashboard in a gesture of affection, thanking God for giving it to me.

Yep, I was totally happy with my car. Like really.

Until I happened to see a shiny, all-power, brand new car.

Then everything changed.

That's when I felt my car was a moving piece of junk.

That's when I noticed that my car's body paint looked more like a jigsaw puzzle.

That's when I realized my car didn't have power windows and power locks.

That's when I discovered my car had grown bumpy and noisy with age.

That's when I felt my car's air-conditioning was feeble.

And then I felt I wasn't a success.

Which was not true, because I could have bought a new car any time I wanted to. But I decided to invest my money in my business first.

If I didn't stop comparing myself, I would have ended resentful of this decision.

I now realize that success must be self-defined.

You need to define success according to your standards — not according to the standards of your neighbor.

If your neighbor has a jet plane in his garage (let's say his name is John Travolta), that doesn't mean you also need a jet plane in your garage to be successful.

Because no matter how rich you become, there'll always be another guy richer than you are.

Take another example.

Do you know that most adultery happens because we start comparing?

Compared to our spouse, for example, that officemate is more affectionate, or this friend is more understanding, or that woman's body is sexier...

And because no husband or wife is perfect, your spouse will always have 90 percent of what you're looking for — but would lack the remaining 10 percent.

So the husband, upon seeing the "other" woman, sees the 10 percent that is missing from his wife — and gets obsessed by it.

He doesn't do anything else but think of that 10 percent.

I want it. I need it. I love it!

But alas, he forgets that his wife has the 90 percent.

And that's what happens when the philandering husband ends up with his mistress. After a few months, a year or two years — Bang! He rudely wakes up to realize he's now holding only 10 percent.

And that he had thrown away the 90 percent he had all along.

Friend, we fall because we forget how wealthy we really are already.

Just an update on my life: Last year, a friend gave me a brand new car. And my old car was given to a missionary priest.

And my wife? I'll never replace her for anything as ugly as brand new.

Define your own success.

Truly Rich Principle:
You are already wealthy.

CHAPTER 58

Give Your Best

You are the only one who knows whether you have won or not. Don't try to be better than someone else. Just be the best that you can be.

— John Wooden's Dad

Let me tell you something absolutely terrible.

My wife told me that in her Catholic high school, they assigned each student to a class based on their previous year's grades. So if you're in section 1, that meant you're bright and the cream of the crop. (Which is where my wife was assigned, by the way.)

Here was the problem. There were eight sections.

Can you imagine what it was like to belong to Section 8?

And here was a bigger problem: Students had IDs hanging around their necks, announcing to the entire universe their name and what section they came from.

I cringe at the idea. I believe labels are powerful, and they determine our future. That plastic laminated ID was worse than branding a cow. It bruised their soul and left marks that would affect their lives forever.

Here's what I find crazy: Schools grade kids according to their academic performance. But research says that there are 30 kinds of intelligences. A kid may be poor in writing or reading but he may be fantastic in mechanical skills, athletics, or the arts. So how dare they label a child "Section 8" based on only one type of intelligence?

I bet some of those Section 8 kids are now 35 years old and working behind some office desk living mediocre unproductive lives because, subconsciously, they still believe they're trapped in Section 8.

The real problem with this entire setup is that *we force the kids to compare their success with others.*

But I repeat: Success has to be self-defined.

For example, I homeschool my son.

Last year, he moved up from Grade 1 to Grade 2.

We had a little ceremony at home with his grandparents.

After a song and prayer, I announced with the voice of a circus emcee, "And now, the First Honor award goes to... Benedict Thomas L. Sanchez!"

My son steps forward, grinning from ear to ear. I drape the large gold medal around his neck. His self-esteem soars.

Obviously, there's no other student. He has no competition. But I believe success must be measured in this way. You don't compete with anyone else.

You only compete with yourself. And as long as you reach your standards, proclaim yourself a success.

Last year, in 2006, we began a homeschool center called the Catholic Filipino Academy to help parents teach their kids at home.[1] This March, we'll have a moving up day for 37 homeschooled kids. Our center makes the actual medals but we've asked the parents to tell us what awards their kids deserve.

If they gave their best, then they have achieved success.

Give your best.

Truly Rich Principle:
Compete with yourself.

[1] For more information on homeschooling, you can write to me at **bosanchez@kerygmafamily.com.** I'll email you an article I wrote on homeschooling.

CHAPTER 59

Your Harvest Will Depend on Your Giving

Money is like manure. If you spread it around, it does a lot of good.
But if you pile it up in one place, it stinks like hell.
— Junior Murchison

People ask me if I'm a prosperity preacher.

I used to frown on all prosperity preachers, lumping them into one box and labeling them heretics.

Not anymore.

Some prosperity preachers are sound.

Some prosperity preachers are indeed unsound, preaching that if we don't live in wealth and health, we simply lack faith.

That's not true and that's not my message. I repeat my message at the beginning of this book: We may be poor because subconsciously we don't want to be rich, because we're financially stupid, and because we're not riding a vehicle to wealth.

But even "heretical" prosperity preachers do a service: *They give people permission to prosper.* They expand their psychological wallet.

So am I a prosperity preacher?

I'm more of a practical preacher.

Usually, prosperity preachers will tell you to do only three things: "If you want to prosper, you've got to (1) Obey God, (2) Believe God, and (3) Give to God."

I remember buying a book by one prosperity preacher on the "16 Steps to Prosperity." I was thrilled that, at last, he'd explain the more practical areas of financial growth — debt management, savings, investments, etc. But when I read his book, all his 16 Steps were mere elaborations of the same three items: Obey, Believe and Give. His Steps? Read God's Word, Reflect on God's Word, Remember God's Word, Do God's Word, Learn to Intercede, Repent of Your Sin, etcetera. He didn't mention anything about the practical steps, such as simplifying your life, saying no to bad debts, gaining financial wisdom, learning how to save, learning how to invest, learning how to create passive income....

Friend, this is the purpose of the book you're holding now.

I wanted to share with you, from a spiritual perspective, the practical things you need to do in order to prosper.

But now that I've shared these practical steps, I now have the license to finally talk to you about "Obeying, Believing and Giving" in this chapter. Because they are incredibly essential to prosperity.

When you give, you act rich. And thus, you're released from scarcity mentality and you develop an abundance mentality within you.

Cardinal Gaudencio Rosales, Archbishop of Manila, launched *Pondo ng Pinoy* to teach people to give. He taught everyone to give 25 centavos a day. Raising money for the poor was only a secondary goal (it has raised a whopping P92.7 million as of December 2006 since it started in June 2004). Its primary goal was creative catechesis — to teach people that they're never too poor to give.

And did you know that secular authors preach on tithing? From Anthony Robins to Robert Kiyosaki, Jack Canfield and Dennis Waitley, these guys insist that people should give 10 percent of their income away.

Why? Because every time I give something away, the entire universe around me scrambles to pay me back in some way. Why? When I give, I create a vacuum in my life — and the universe hates a vacuum. It will rush in and fill it to overflowing.

That's my belief.

The reward of giving isn't arithmetic. If I give a mango, I don't receive another mango. Instead, the reward of giving is exponential. I receive a mango tree.

If I give a mango, I'm planting my mango seed on the soil of God's universe, and so I receive an entire mango tree with potentially thousands of fruits inside it.

So my harvest is determined by my giving. The more I give, the more I receive. It's a law written in the very fabric of the universe.

And this has been my experience.

At the start of my book, I shared that I've now reached a point where I give 40 percent of my income away. I also shared that my goal is to do a reverse-tithe, to give 90 percent of my income away.

Why? Because I believe that the ultimate purpose of money is to love others.

And God has rewarded me beyond my wildest imagination.

Make a decision now — how much will you give to God each month.

For centuries, people tithe or give 10 percent of their income. Start with that.

You will be blessed.

No doubt about it.

Your harvest will be determined by your giving.

Truly Rich Principle:
The more I give, the more I receive. This is a law written in the very fabric of the universe.

CHAPTER 60

Sacrifice Your Wealth for Others

Poverty is abandonment. We have abandoned the poor.
— Tony Meloto

Something wonderful is happening.

I met Esok and Sally Adraneda in Chicago and they did something that I don't see very often: The couple sold their five-bedroom home, bought a smaller house, and gave the proceeds to Gawad Kalinga to build one entire GK village of hundreds of homes for the poorest of the poor. Not content with that, they also sold their Mercedes Benz and gave all the proceeds to GK. What was mere luxury for one family are now homes to hundreds of very poor families.

Greg Monteclaro did the same thing. He sold his brand new BMW to build 100 GK homes for the poor.

The Concepcion family are making helping the poor a family affair. Industrialist Joe Concepcion, the head of the clan, his son Joey Concepcion III, president of RFM, his other son John Concepcion, president of Selecta — together with their wives and children and grandchildren — are building hundreds of homes for the poor *with their own hands.*

I talked to Tony Meloto, the dreamer that started it all. He explained the core problem in these words. "We don't see the poor as *our* family. So we're satisfied with charity. But if we see the poor as *our* family, we won't give charity. We'll love them. We'll shed our blood."

Friend, there's a great miracle happening across the country and it's called Gawad Kalinga. It's the most fantastic thing I have ever seen in a long time.

As of this writing, Gawad Kalinga has built 840 villages across the country consisting of thousands of beautiful, colorful homes for the poor. They are built *for* the poor, built *with* the poor, and built *by* the poor. No, it isn't another dole out program. The poor own it, paid by their sweat. They build each other's homes. They pave their streets.

They plant each other's gardens and picket fences. And these villages are gorgeous. So pretty, some are tourist attractions!

That's not all. There are now thousands of poor families in these GK villages who have tiny businesses — from *sari-sari* stores, handicrafts, bananacues, rice retailing — capitalized by their very unique cooperatives.

And there's more. In these same areas, they've organized preschools for impoverished kids, complete with a free meal each day. There are out-of-school teenagers, who instead of becoming tomorrow's kidnappers, thieves and drug pushers, are now scholars in schools, joining prayer groups and serving God.

And that's what makes this whole thing work: The poor are getting to know God in a deeper way. Prayer meetings, value formation classes, and spiritual seminars are being conducted every day in these same villages.

All these wonderful things are happening because a few ordinary human beings are shedding their blood for the poor. Yes, these nameless heroes are willing to die for the poor — giving time, energy and money to create this miracle.

Tony said something else that blew my mind. He said, "When God called me to do this work, He asked me to send to the poor what was most precious to me. So I sent my 16-year-old daughter to serve in the slum areas. People said I was insane!" Because there she was, surrounded by violent gang fighting, drug addicts and kidnappers.

But Tony won their trust, and today, all his four children continue to work with the poor in the slums. But the gangs and drug addicts are no longer there. They have been converted to the Lord and are now serving God as well.

I've become a proud partner with Gawad Kalinga.[1]

Together with my organizations and many others, we're building a GK village in Montalban, Rizal. It's exciting to be part of God's miracle in the country.

Friend, this is the ultimate message of the entire book.

There's no point in becoming wealthy for wealth's sake. That path will only lead to emptiness and despair.

[1] For more information on Gawad Kalinga, go to **www.gawadkalinga.org**

We receive blessings to bless others.
We receive wealth so that we can give it away.

Sacrifice your wealth for the poor.

Truly Rich Principle:
If you see the poor as your family, you won't give charity. You'll love them. You'll shed your blood for them.

EPILOGUE

Get a Champion Partner

I have come that you may have life and have it in abundance.
— John 10:10

I'm not a great badminton player.

Oh, I do own a nice racket — given by my friend Arun Gogna.

I also own a nifty pair of yellow badminton shoes.

And I play once in a while. (Okay, that's not true. How about every time Haley's comet passes by?)

One day, my friend Mike Joseph invited me to play.

Mike is an expert badminton player who's been playing for 40 years.

So I went to the gym to get some training from him when he shocked me and said, "Let's play doubles. You'll be my partner."

"Uh, Mike, uh… can I know who'll be our opponents?"

"Don't worry. Class B players."

"What does that mean? If by that you mean quadriplegics strapped in wheelchairs with spastic muscular disorders who can only hold their badminton rackets with their lips, I'm game."

"Class B players are very good players, but they're not champions yet," he said.

"Mike! I'm no good!" I began hyperventilating, "I guarantee you'll be embarrassed because you'll lose on account of me!" The truth was, I wasn't thinking of him at all. I was thinking of my own shame.

"Bo, I want you to stand in front of the court," He pointed to the net. I took my place two feet away from the net and asked, "Here?"

"Yes. If you see the ball coming near you, hit it hard."

"That's it? And if it's not near me?"

"I'll take care of the rest."

So that's how the game went.

In the entire 15-minute game, I hit the shuttlecock twice. Twice! The rest of the time, Mike was all over the place swatting balls. And when I say all over, I mean all over. He was like The Flash of the Justice League of America. Zoom here and zoom there, and smash the ball here and smash the ball there.

When Mike's dead, I'll be one of his witnesses to sainthood. Because I saw the gift of bilocation right there. Because I'd see him on my left, and in a split second, I'd see him on my right. Man, he was good.

In other words, we won 15-2.

Yes, the two points of the opponent were courtesy of you know who.

When we were sitting on the bench, reveling in our victory, I told him, "Mike, did you like how I guarded the net? Fantastic, huh?"

"Yeah," Mike said, "no one stole it. It's still there."

Can I be honest with you?

I've been winning a lot of games in my life. My spiritual life is strong. My family life is intimate. My work is fantastic. And yes, my finances are growing year after year.

Blame my Champion Partner.

Like Mike, I feel His presence everywhere I go. He's all over the place.

He takes care of all my missed shots.

All He asks is that I be His Partner.

And the rest is victory.

Friend, do you really want to be truly rich?

Get a Champion Partner.

I remain your friend,

Bo Sanchez

P.S. I want to give you two of my inspiring E-books that will help you grow in your personal life — for FREE! Log on to www.bosanchez.ph. When you do, you also get The Bo Sanchez Soulfood Letter in your inbox each week — to inspire you to succeed in life.

P.S.2. Do you want to watch inspiring videos that will help you grow and manifest the goodness in you? Watch my daily "reality show" and other powerful talks on the Internet at www.preacherinbluejeans.com.

P.S.3. I've started a global, borderless, non-physical community called **www.kerygmafamily.com.** If you want a mountain-load of great stuff for your spiritual growth, FREE, sign up — and get a chance to also support my ministry. (More information on the next page.)

By Joining the Kerygma Family, You Will Receive a Mountain of Blessings for Your Spiritual Life

Here's what will happen to you when you join the Kerygma Family:

1. You'll receive daily Bible reflections for your spiritual growth.
2. Each month, you'll get to read an online copy of *Kerygma,* the #1 Catholic inspirational magazine in the Philippines.
3. You'll belong to a borderless, global, non-physical community spread all over the world connected through prayer and the desire for personal growth.
4. You shall have the special privilege of supporting this expansive work of the Lord (totally optional!), which includes Anawim, a ministry for the poorest of the poor, the abandoned elderly; Shepherd's Voice, a media ministry that uses TV, radio, print, and the Internet to broadcast God's love to spiritually hungry people worldwide.
5. You and your intentions shall be included in our intercession team's prayers.

The KERYGMA Family

To join the KerygmaFamily,
log on to **www.kerygmafamily.com**

Don't delay!

APPENDIX:

How Financially Healthy Are You?

The Lord will grant you abundant prosperity... The Lord will open the heavens, the storehouse of his bounty, to send rain on your land in season and to bless all the work of your hands. You will lend to many nations but will borrow from none.

— Deuteronomy 28:11-12

Are you financially sick or healthy?

It depends on how many steps you've taken towards financial health.

As a way of review, I will share with you the Six Steps to Financial Health. If you notice, I put a Step 0 because this is a faith act. How can a poor person give? But that is the challenge. When he becomes generous, he attracts more generosity upon his life. Here they are:

Step 0: Give to God a Monthly Love Offering (Start with 10 percent)

This is the purpose of money — to use it for love. And tithing is the "training wheels" to learn how to do this. Each month, set aside a fixed percentage of your income to God and the poor. And be open to the blessings that will flow to you.

Step 1: Free Yourself from All Bad Debt

List down all your bad debts and declare when your Freedom Day will be. Never borrow for anything that doesn't put money into your pocket. Renegotiate with creditors if you have to.

Step 2: Increase Your Income and Start a Sideline

Grow yourself, your skills and your abilities. In your job, be known as someone who works fast. Always get more responsibilities. ("Sir, I finished the project. Is there anything else you want me to do?") Your boss will be forced to promote you. And sell something on the side and keep on learning.

Step 3: Get Protection (Insurance) Equal to 10 Times Your Annual Expenses
Your goal is to be self-insured. But while your investments haven't reached that point where your passive income is equal or greater than your expenses, you need to buy insurance.

Step 4: Create an Emergency Fund in the Bank Equal to Six Months' Expenses
These are for your daily expenses as well as unforeseen expenses. Having an Emergency Fund prevents you from dipping into your long-term retirement fund.

Step 5: Create a Retirement Fund Saving 20 Percent of Your Monthly Income in Various Growth Funds
Keep researching on the best places you can put your long-term savings. It will be determined by your age and the level of risk you're comfortable with.

Step 6: Create Passive Income via Businesses and Investments Equal to or More Than Your Expenses
This is financial freedom. It is the place where, even if you stop working, you can still live your present lifestyle.

As you take one step after another step, you gain in financial health.

Friend, this book is only a start of your exciting journey towards material and spiritual abundance.

Keep learning. Read books on money. Attend seminars on money. Get mentors and financial coaches.

Remember: You create your future by your choice today!

References:

Robert Allen, *Multiple Income Streams*
Jack Canfield, *The Success Principles*
T. Harv Eker, *Secrets of the Millionaire Mind*
Larry Gamboa, *Think Rich, Pinoy!*
Larry Gamboa, *Grow Rich, Pinoy!*
Robert Kiyosaki, *Rich Dad, Poor Dad*
Thomas Stanley, *The Millionaire Next Door*

Do You Want Passive Income?

Learn up-to-date, cutting-edge information on how you can make your money work for you and create passive income. Receive 3 FREE Issues of Bo Sanchez' *Truly Rich Financial Newsletter*. In it, you will find...

- Advice on where to put your money for long-term growth
- How to know if an investment is good or not good
- Marketing strategies that will consistently grow your small business
- What are the wrong financial habits that rob you of your wealth
- How to remain spiritually strong as your money increases
- So much more!

Log on to **www.iamtrulyrich.com** and receive 3 FREE Issues of Bo Sanchez' Truly Rich Financial Newsletter. Or call up our office at (632) 722-9562 now. Don't miss this great storehouse of financial wisdom that can save you from financial ruin and misery.

Get Ready for Abundance!

Bo Sanchez and his Team of Financial Experts hold transformational "Truly Rich Seminars" that will deepen, strengthen, and help you apply the powerful truths you learned in this book. Step-by-step, Bo and his team will take you through the journey towards true financial and spiritual freedom.

Listening to Bo and his team will change the way you think, enlarge your psychological wallet and prepare you to receive abundance into your life.

If you attend the seminar, you shall automatically become a member of Bo Sanchez's Truly Rich Club.

For dates and venue, log on to **www.iamtrulyrich.com** or call up our office at (632) 722-9562 or email us at **beaconlightevents@gmail.com.**

About the Author

Bo Sanchez is the author of 25 bestselling books and publisher of eight periodicals. Bo also has a weekly TV show, a daily radio program, and a daily Internet show. He travels extensively around the world as a powerful speaker. So far, he has addressed audiences in 14 countries, including 37 cities in North America. His Soulfood blog is read each week by more than a hundred thousand people. You can read his blog at www.BoSanchez.ph and watch his video blog at www.PreacherInBlueJeans.com

He founded many organizations, such as Anawim, a special home for the abandoned elderly, and Shepherd's Voice, a media group that publishes the widest-read inspirational literature in the country. He also founded an international, borderless, virtual, on-line community called www.KerygmaFamily.com that helps people grow in their spiritual life.

Bo received The Outstanding Young Men (TOYM) Award for 2006 and the Serviam Award, the highest recognition given by CMMA or Catholic Mass Media Awards.

Privately, Bo is also a micro-entrepreneur. He engages in small business and real estate not only for his family's needs and for his various projects, but also from his firm belief that one of the most important solutions to his country's economic problems is to raise up more micro-entrepreneurs among his countrymen. He frequently teaches and writes about financial literacy, believing that our poverty is hugely a product of people's low financial I.Q. on subjects such as debt-management, saving, investing and business. He writes the TrulyRich Letter at www.IAmTrulyRich.com to help people grow in their financial life and spiritual life at the same time.

In another endeavor he's passionate about, Bo started the Catholic Filipino Academy to help parents who want to teach their children at home. For more information, log on to www.CatholicFilipinoAcademy.com

But above all these, Bo believes that his first call is to be a loving husband to his wife, Marowe, and a devoted father to his sons, Benedict and Francis. They live in Manila, Philippines.

Other books in the Simplify Series

Simplify and Create Abundance

Chapter one of Simplify and Live the Good Life

By Bo Sanchez

1
LIVE FROM THE CORE OF YOUR BEING

It is not enough if you are busy.
The question is, what are you busy about?
—Henry David Thoreau

Happiness is not found outside of you. It doesn't come from cars, clothes, cash or Caribbean cruises. Happiness is found within.

But how can you find it if you don't have the simplicity of time and space to discover the most important things in your life? How can you search the depths of your soul if you are too busy impressing others, acquiring wealth, protecting your properties and paying your debts?

Simplicity is not about the externals either: living in a doghouse, eating in a hepatitis joint or wearing rags.

The best definition of simplicity I have ever read comes from Janet Luhrs's book, The Simple Living Guide. There she says that simplicity is living from the core of your being.

I cannot agree more.

I believe that simplicity is having the time and space to embrace what is most important to you. It is having the leisure to cherish it, having the freedom to glory in it, and having the power to live by it.

Along the way, you'll discover that the most important things in life aren't things but the persons who have become part of your lives. But that's something you'll have to discover yourself.

Give up shallowness.

Live from the core of your being.

Action Plan

Get a notebook and begin a journal for this book. Write down your discoveries, insights, reflections and action plan for each chapter. What is your core? What are the most important things in your life right now? Do you allow your core to direct and empower your daily decisions and actions?

Chapter one of *Simplify and Create Abundance*

By Bo Sanchez

1
DEFINE SUCCESS IN YOUR OWN TERMS

Nothing is more simple than greatness;
indeed, to be simple is to be great.
—Ralph Waldo Emerson

When I was 13 years old, I looked like the perfect loser.

Because I wanted to imitate St. Francis of Assisi, I wore a crummy old tee shirt, walked in cheap worn-out sandals, and had the muscular heft of a praying mantis. I never combed my hair or put on deodorant. Yet even at that time, I was already leading small prayer meetings, feeding the poor in the streets and having the time of my life.

I believe that in the eyes of God, this perfect loser was a great success.

When I was 20 years old, I didn't look as pathetic anymore. I learned that wearing presentable clothes and putting on deodorant made more people listen to my preaching — as the deodorant prevented them from fainting all the time. Though still penniless as the rat in my mother's kitchen, I was preaching from town to town, city to city, and country to country — bringing only God's love and my toothbrush with me.

And yes, I believe I was a great success as well.

Today, I'm still serving God with the same passion — preaching, writing, running dynamic organizations and pioneering new things for the Kingdom. I'm now married and have a family, and thus can no longer be penniless. I'm experiencing Simple Abundance and earning more than enough to be generous.

I know God thinks I'm a great success.

It's so easy to buy into the success gospel of the world. I'm not going to argue that success is important. But who says success has one definition?

Is success fat bank accounts, vacation houses, Rolexes and Jaguars?

Or is it a heart that loves and laughs and shares and cares?

Define success in your terms.

ACTION PLAN

Think. How do you define success? What are the things that should happen to you for you to say you're a great success? Write this down.

Happy Birthday
Patrick!
Papa
10/17/13

SHEPHERD'S VOICE

Learn to live a fantastic life
Log on to www.bosanchez.ph